ADVANCED VEHICLE STOP TACTICS

Skills for Today's Survival Conscious Officer

Written by a Patrolman for Patrol Officers

Michael T. Rayburn

Foreword by David M. Grossi
Former Senior Instructor, Calibre Press, Inc.

43-08 162nd Street
Flushing, NY 11358
www.LooseleafLaw.com
800-647-5547

1st Printing 2002
2nd Printing 2005
3rd Printing 2010
4th Printing 2011
5th Printing 2013

Library of Congress Cataloging-in-Publication Data

Rayburn, Michael T., 1959-
Advanced vehicle stop tactics : skills for today's survival conscious officer / by Michael T. Rayburn
p. cm.
Includes index.
ISBN 1-889031-45-3
1. Traffic police--United States--Handbooks, manuals, etc. 2. Traffic safety--United States--Handbooks, manuals, etc. 3. Traffic violations--United States--Handbooks, manuals, etc. 4. Law enforcement--United States--Safety measures--Handbooks, manuals, etc. 5. Arrest (Police methods)--United States--Handbooks, manuals, etc. 6.Police--Violence against--United States--Prevention. I. Title.

HV8079.P5 R38 2001
363.2'332'0973--dc21

00-067840

Printed in United States of America

Cover design by *Sans Serif*, Saline, Michigan

This book is dedicated to Exine May Rayburn,
a devoted mother and ardent reader, who loved books
and always encouraged me to read,
and to B.C. for all of your help and support over the years.

Special thanks to Deputy Michael Garavelli (the bad guy), Officers Paul Veitch and Patrick O'Leary and Investigator Robert Jillson who assisted me with the pictures for this book.

Foreword

It was an honor to have been asked to write the foreword for Mike Rayburn's first book on this most important topic of vehicle stop tactics. There has never been a more important time in law enforcement for a thorough authoritative text on the topic of vehicle stop tactics. *Advanced Vehicle Stop Tactics* is must reading for every street officer. According to the latest FBI statistics, one in ten physical attacks against police officers occurs while engaged in traffic stops or vehicle pursuits. The fact is that of police officers who get killed making vehicle stops, most die making low risk stops for what they perceived to be minor traffic violations. It is also a fact that to date, the names of more than 300 police officers who have been killed making vehicle stops are engraved on the rough granite walls of National Law Enforcement Officers Memorial in Washington, D.C.

Today's highways are not unlike our individual towns and cities, with each car, SUV, minivan or semi-truck carrying what could be evidence of a crime. While most citizens, and more than a few street cops, think that high risk (or felony) stops pose the greatest risk for police officers, it's actually the low risk (or unknown) vehicle stop that is the most dangerous of the two. Why? Because most often, officers are stopping subjects they know almost nothing about. In this text, Mike Rayburn, a career police officer, not only educates today's law enforcement professionals on the importance of effective and safe vehicle stop tactics, he also touches on some very important and usually ignored areas such as how to clear campers, buses, vans and SUVs, semi-trucks and motorcycles. In his chapter on Clearing the Vehicle, Mike discusses a concept he calls the "horizontal angle of incidence," the vehicular version of "slicing the pie." He also shares the latest information on bullet deflection and how laminated windshield glass differs from the tempered glass normally used in side and rear vehicle windows. He also gives considerable time to the technique of shooting through your own windshield, taking the angle of deflection into consideration.

There are no war stories or self-aggrandizing tales of street escapades contained in the following 100+ pages. However, what is inside the covers of this manual are more than 50 diagrams and photographs that will aid the officer in mastering the tactics Mike

Rayburn discusses. While you may not totally agree with every tactic or technique Mike discusses or describes, keep an open mind and you're guaranteed to learn something new.

All in all, *Advanced Vehicle Stops Tactics*, in my opinion, is one of the most well-researched, thorough, comprehensive, easy to read, and easy to understand manuals on how to conduct vehicle stops. Enjoy and learn!

David M. Grossi, Former Senior Instructor
Calibre Press, Inc.
Street Survival Seminars

Table of Contents

Low/Unknown Risk Stops

Traffic stops are a necessary part of any Police Officer's job. Whether it's to enforce a simple traffic violation or to investigate a crime, all traffic stops have the potential for danger. For this reason your tactics must always be guided by common sense while maintaining officer safety at all times.

Every year officers are injured and sometimes killed at traffic stops. Whether it's through the dangerous actions of inattentive or reckless drivers in passing vehicles or the deliberate acts of assault and murder perpetrated by depraved individuals within our society. According to FBI statistics one in ten physical attacks against a Law Enforcement Officer occurs while engaged in a traffic stop or pursuit.

Because no two traffic stops are ever the same it would be impossible to cover every situation that an officer may encounter at a traffic stop. A certain vehicle stop tactic may or may not work for you. It may be because of the locale or terrain in which you work, the resources that are available to you, or just your own personal preference as to how you stop and approach a vehicle.

This manual is to be considered as a general guideline only. You may find it necessary to vary these procedures in order to adjust to your unique situation. If you decide to adjust a particular tactic to fit your circumstances think before you act.

Keep in mind that every vehicle stop can escalate from a Low/Unknown Risk situation to a High Risk Stop in a matter of seconds. Remember the Concept of Contact & Cover, and use it. Anytime an officer stops a vehicle it must always be based on reasonable and probable cause. There must be a legitimate reason for the traffic stop and officers must be able to explain and articulate the violation or behavior that prompted the stop. Your tactics will vary depending on the severity of the offense and whether the stop is occurring in the daylight or in the dark.

Generally a Low/Unknown Risk Stop can be divided into two basic categories:

1. Traffic violation or traffic enforcement: red light violation, speeding, etc.

2. Investigative stops: suspicious activity, possible BOLO information, etc.

Low/Unknown Risk Stop Techniques

Initial Procedures

1. The officer must always be able to articulate the reason for the stop whether the stop was for a traffic violation or an investigative stop. If you are in a two-officer unit make sure that your partner is aware of the reason for the stop before proceeding any further. Communications with your partner is very important and must be maintained at all times. Contact and cover must also be maintained at all times.
2. Write down the license tag number and a brief description of the vehicle. This is done in case you become incapacitated and unable to communicate. Having this information written down somewhere in your patrol car will assist your fellow officers in capturing your assailant.
3. Check the vehicle license against the hot sheet and run the license via the car radio or the MDT (mobile data terminal). If you are a single officer unit the license tag will be checked through dispatch via the car radio. The officer needs to maintain visual contact with the violator and should not be distracted by the MDT computer screen. If the stop is occurring at night the computer screen will impair the officer's night vision.
4. Hold off on activating your emergency lights or closing the distance on the vehicle. Instead watch the occupants movements. Watching a person's shoulders and head will give you an indication of whether they are reaching for something. If the subject reaches for a weapon or attempts to hide contraband under the seat or in the glove box one of his shoulders will dip (or drop) downwards. If the subject reaches into the center console his shoulder will raise up. Any twisting of the upper torso may indicate he is reaching for a weapon in his waistband.
5. Consider where you want to stop the vehicle. You want the tactical advantages to be on your side.

6. Notify dispatch of your position and activity as well as the license number and description of the vehicle and it's occupant(s). If you are going to need additional resources (backup, K-9) now is the time to notify dispatch.
7. Your description of the vehicle should include any unique descriptors. Unique descriptors include bumper stickers, damage to the vehicle or any other unique characteristics of the vehicle.
8. Your description of the occupants should be the same. Example: Two white males wearing dark clothing and ball caps, one with red hair.

Stopping Location

1. Try to stop the vehicle in a legal location out of the flow of traffic. Do not stop vehicles on the left side of the roadway. You may have to guide (from behind) these vehicles over to the right side of the roadway using your public address (PA) system.
2. Avoid conducting the stop on hillcrests, at intersections, in alleys or any other area that may pose a hazard to you or other motorist. Remember that you control the stop.
3. Avoid stopping vehicles near militant (or gang) hangouts, unruly groups or near other hostile environments.
4. Try to perform the stop in an area that is well illuminated.
5. Choose an area that has a safe background for shooting should the officer have to use deadly force.
6. Choose an area that is familiar to you.
7. If you don't like the area where the violator has stopped his vehicle, get on the PA system and direct the vehicle to another location.

Pullover Procedures

1. Before you attempt to stop the vehicle know your location and direction of travel. Any call can take a turn for the worse in a matter of seconds. For this reason you should always know where you are and in which direction you are headed in.
2. When you are in a suitable location and close enough to control the stop activate all of your emergency lighting to include your

wigwags and spotlight. Even in daylight these lights will somewhat dazzle and disorient the subject. If the stop is occurring at night do not activate your spotlight until the subject's vehicle has come to an almost complete stop. The spotlight will make it difficult for the operator of the vehicle to see. However, in some cases you can use this tactic to your advantage by making it difficult for the operator to see.

3. Give short blasts on your siren switching back and forth between the siren and the PA (public address system) mode. This will allow the PA system to be on in case you need it.
4. **Command Presence:** Take control of the traffic stop by the use of command presence. By activating your lights and siren together the violator's attention is immediately directed to you. This lets the violator know who is in charge of the traffic stop. If you've ever read or watched videos of some of the interviews with convicted cop killers you will realize several familiar comments made by the killers. The one that is often stated by a number of these individuals is that the officer failed to take charge of the situation or used less force than the suspects themselves would have used if they were the officers in the same spot. This tactical flaw can be remedied through the use of command presence. Right from the start let the violator know that you are in charge by activating your lights and siren together at the same time. This signals to the operator of the vehicle that you are in charge and you want them to stop now! Take control of the stop. Don't let the violator dictate to you what tactics you will use. This doesn't mean that you be rude or overly aggressive but that you take charge of the stop through your actions and your commanding voice. Some community policing advocates may feel that this tactic is a little overbearing. But it's better to be a little overbearing than to have your brother and sister officers watch a jailhouse interview with your killer explaining how you failed to take charge of him at a traffic stop.
5. Watch the occupants at all times. Look for contraband being discarded or furtive movements by the occupants. Look for the dipping or raising of the shoulders.
6. Be cautious of any sudden stops by the violator's vehicle. A growing tactic being used among street gangs is to abruptly stop

their vehicle so the police cruiser is forced to stop suddenly and too closely. The suspect then rapidly reverses his vehicle into the cruiser activating the airbag. Thereby disabling the police vehicle. The vehicle can still be driven but only with a great deal of difficulty because the now deflated airbag is sitting in the officer's lap.

Positioning Your Vehicle

Over the years various tactics have been developed which incorporate positioning your police vehicle at different angles and at different distances from the violator's vehicle. Actual studies have been conducted where police vehicles were crashed to determine which method was the safest position for your vehicle. Only one position offers the officer the best protection from rear end collisions or from any assaults from the occupants of the vehicle, as well as affording the best visibility of the rearward facing emergency lighting to any vehicles approaching from behind. For this reason only onc vehicle position will be discussed. Once the police vehicle is positioned properly it is the tactics used from that point forward that can be changed or altered.

1. **Left Offset:** Offset the police vehicle approximately 2' – 3' to the left lining up the center of your hood with the left rear fender of the vehicle and 15' – 25' (or 1 – 1½ car lengths) behind the violator's vehicle. A general rule of thumb is to pull far enough back to be able to see the violator's rear tires touching the pavement.
2. Remember that distance is our ally. The further back you are the more reaction time you will have. Staying further back also allows you to see more of the vehicle. This is beneficial when dealing with larger vehicles such as vans, SUV's or tractor-trailers. However, too far back and you won't be able to control the stop and it will make it difficult to retreat to your vehicle for cover if you should come under fire.
3. This position allows the rear of the police vehicle to absorb most low speed impacts from a rear end collision keeping the passenger compartment in tact.

4. Do not turn your wheels to one side or the other. If your vehicle was to get hit from behind it will send your vehicle hurling in the direction the wheels were turned. Which could prove fatal if you were in it's path while walking up to or back from the violator's vehicle.
5. It also provides a safety zone for the officer when he is out of the vehicle.
6. If you find you have stopped to close to the violator's vehicle wait until the subject's vehicle has almost come to a complete stop and then reverse your police vehicle to a comfortable distance. If anyone in the violator's vehicle was to exit rapidly continue reversing to a safe location. (see the **coming under fire** section of this manual)

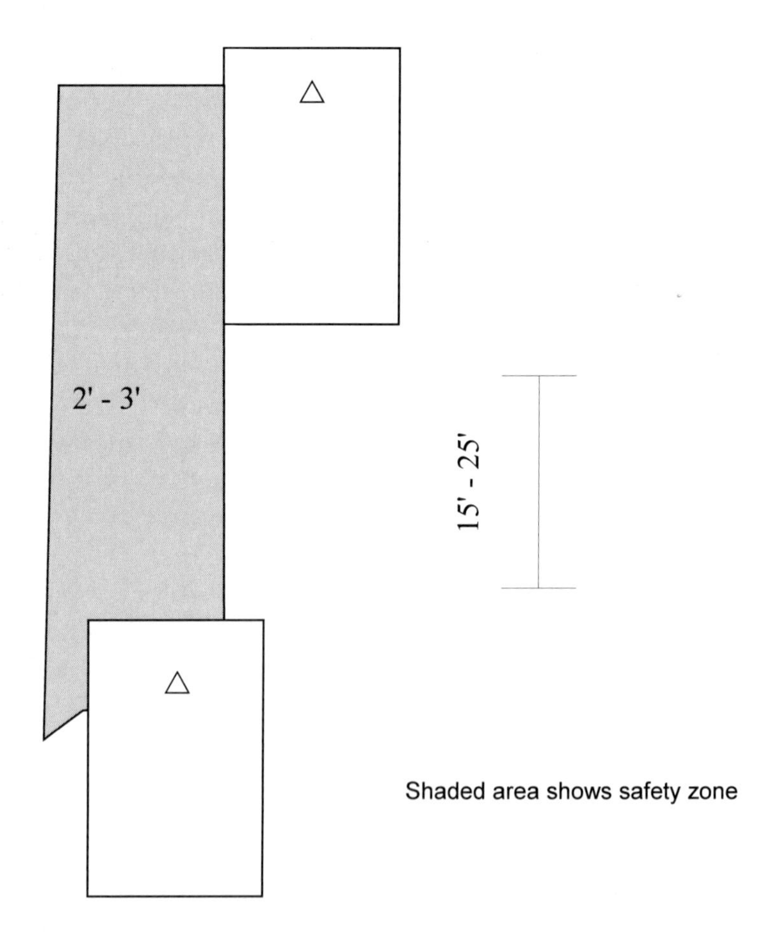

Shaded area shows safety zone

Pre-Exit

1. Remember to roll down your windows and unlock your doors so any backup or cover officers will have access to your vehicle for cover and or equipment.
2. Turn on your portable radio before you exit your cruiser. There's nothing worse than to be calling for help with your portable turned off.
3. Always bring your police baton. You work within a use of force continuum, which includes the use of impact weapons (baton). When you need your baton it will be to late to stop and go back to the car to get it. Juries do not want to hear that you escalated your use of force because you didn't bring the proper equipment that was issued to you.
4. Always bring your flashlight with you on all stops even during the day. You never know where a foot chase will lead you.

Exiting Your Vehicle

1. Quickly check for traffic before exiting your vehicle. Then exit the vehicle immediately and take a guarding position standing behind your door. Take time to observe the occupants of the vehicle.
2. You want to be out of the vehicle as quickly as possible. By doing this you give yourself more options for cover should you come under attack.
3. Leave the door to you police vehicle open. This will give you some added protection by forcing any vehicles to go around the door. It will widen your safety zone as you approach the violator's vehicle. Some Chiefs may get upset at this tactic. Remind them that it's cheaper to buy a new door than it is to replace an officer. Place a wide piece of reflective tape on the inside of the door. This will make the door more visible to traffic. Some newer model cruisers have a reflector built into the inside of the door panel. Leaving the door open also slows any traffic approaching from the rear. When the operator of a vehicle approaching from the rear sees the open door they will think that an officer may be emerging from the police vehicle and will automatically slow

down. The next time you're on a busy highway with traffic zooming by try this tactic and you'll see for yourself that it slows the traffic down.

Approach

There are a number of options that are available to the officer. The choice will depend on the circumstances and the location of the stop and whether the stop is occurring in daylight hours or in the dark. The decision on which particular stop to deploy is the officer's discretion. Any combination of these tactics can be utilized by the officer(s). The officer may also elect to change from one approach to another in midstream, remaining flexible to the ever-changing world we work in.

Basic Left Side Approach (Daytime)

1. In this approach the contact officer will approach the suspect vehicle on the driver's side of the vehicle.
2. A number of tactics have been used to check the trunk to insure it is closed. Some involve pushing down on the trunk while others involve pulling up on the trunk. Both will give the officer's position away. Also with most cars now a days having interior trunk release mechanisms these tactics are obsolete. A better tactic is to just run your finger along the seam of the trunk. If it is ajar the officer will feel the unevenness of the seam. If you feel that the trunk is ajar, quickly back away and seek cover. Call for backup and use the "call out" approach to call the driver back to your location. Once the driver is back to your location, question him as to the contents of the trunk. You may want to consider lightly placing your hand on the trunk leaving a palm print behind. In case the unspeakable occurs this print will help convict your assailants.
3. The contact officer should position himself behind the doorjamb to avoid being struck by the door. By staying a little further back than you would normally stand the officer is not only able to avoid being struck by the door but he is one step closer to the rear of the vehicle should he have to move to seek cover. Some

officers who work on busy highways prefer to stand forward of the vehicle so they can see the occupants and watch traffic at the same time. This position is not recommended. If the officer were to come under fire the only places he could move to would be back past the offender, out into traffic or in front of the violator's vehicle. All three put the officer at a higher risk. This is one of the reasons why the left offset is the recommended positioning of your vehicle. Force traffic around you so you don't have to worry about it. If you have to step forward of the door to check the VIN or registration/inspection stickers do so by pivoting your body. This is accomplished by first having the operator place his hands on the steering wheel or on the dash. Have any occupants place their hands on the dashboard. If you feel the need have any rear seat passengers place their hands on their heads. For a right handed officer his left side should already be forward with his right side towards the back of the vehicle. The officer simple takes a large step with his left foot and then pivots around backward to his right. This will insure that his gun side is always facing away from and out of the reach of the driver of the vehicle. The officer can then safely verify any information while keeping an eye on the occupant's movements. To go back to his position behind the doorjamb the officer simply takes a large step with his left foot and then pivots forward with his right side. This will again keep his weapon out of the reach of the driver.

4. If a second officer is available to act as a cover officer have him stand at the right rear (passenger side) of the vehicle. If personal cover is available (lamp post, telephone pole, etc.) the cover officer should stand near enough to it to be able to reach it in one step should a gun fight break out.
5. The contact officer obtains all required documentation (driver license, vehicle registration, etc.). Should the suspect vehicle contain any passengers in the rear seat, the contact officer can instruct the driver to pass any required documentation back to the passenger to be handed to the officer. If the officer feels he needs to speak to the operator on a one to one basis, such as checking for possible intoxication, then the officer should have the driver exit the vehicle for further investigation rather than passing by any rear seat passengers. While obtaining documentation watch

the suspects hands and any furtive movements by the occupants. Don't read the information while the suspect is moving.

6. Advise the driver of the violation or reason for the stop. The person may not have any idea why you are stopping him. Also on drug interdiction stops this will put the driver at ease so you can continue your investigation.
7. Ask the driver if there was some reason for him to commit the violation. This allows the driver to vent his frustration for being stopped. Most drivers are not mad at you they are just mad at getting caught. Allowing them to vent their frustration diffuses the situation. They are looking for someone to hear their excuse, no matter how lame it is. Try this tactic out for yourself and you'll soon have people thanking you when you hand them their citation. They are not thanking you for the ticket, they are thanking you for being polite and courteous and for allowing them to tell their side of the story as to why they committed the violation. Their "side of the story" should be documented to be used later in court against them.

   This tactic will help you to avoid those annoying personnel complaints that arise out of traffic stops. The majority of citizen complaints against officers at traffic stops are for rudeness. By allowing them to tell their "side of the story" the citizen feels that the officer was courteous and "heard them out" as to why they committed the violation.
8. Avoid telling the operator that you will be issuing him a ticket. This will anger some people and they will attempt to argue with you over the issuance of the citation. The side of the road is no place for a legal argument. That's what the courts are for. Instead, tell the operator that you are going back to your vehicle to verify the information that he has given you and ask him to wait in his vehicle for you.

   At this point the operator will still have some hope that he can talk you out of the ticket. When you return to the vehicle with the citation, he will realize that it's too late for any arguments.
9. Do not write the citation at the suspect vehicle. Return to your police vehicle to write any citations. Remember to glance over your shoulder as you are returning to your vehicle. Trying to walk backward to your vehicle is too dangerous of a task. You could

trip and fall, (making you look like an idiot) or you could walk backward right into the path of an oncoming vehicle. Walk forward to your vehicle glancing over your shoulder several times.

10. Sit in the passenger side of your vehicle to write the citation. If you sit in the driver's seat to write the ticket you are stuck between the center equipment stack/console and the traffic outside your door. By sitting in the passenger seat you can move more safely and quickly out of the vehicle and to cover if need be.
11. The cover officer remains at the suspect vehicle while the citation is being written. This is to insure your safety while writing the ticket.
12. If no cover officer is available consider moving your vehicle backward approximately one car length while you write the ticket. This will give you more reaction distance should someone exit the vehicle to launch an attack against you. It also allows you to see more of the vehicle and more of the area around the vehicle.
13. If a signature is required advise the suspect that his signature is only a promise to appear. Never advise the suspect of the amount of the fine. This could trigger a violent reaction from the suspect should he think that the fine is excessive.

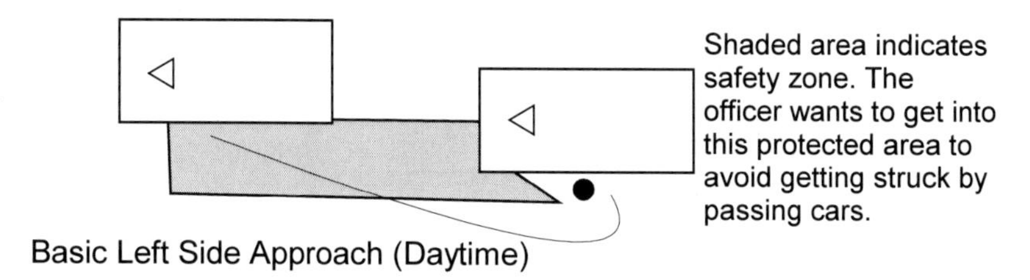

Basic Left Side Approach (Daytime)

Basic Right Side Approach (Daytime)

The basic right side approach has been around for a few years now. It was first developed to give the officer an option to the old standard of walking up to the driver's side window. This procedure has a number of tactical benefits to it when used properly. However, it is not a cure all and should not be used all of the time.

Some of the basic tactics remain the same such as inspecting the trunk and how to deal with rear seat passengers.

1. The officer positions his vehicle in the left offset position.

2. The officer exits his vehicle leaving the door open and walks around the back of the cruiser. He then approaches the violator's vehicle on the right side. For obvious reasons do not cross in between your vehicle and the violator's.
3. The benefit of this approach is that it keeps the officer out of the flow of traffic. Should the officer come under fire he can quickly move to some cover and not have to worry about running out into traffic. (see the coming under fire section)
4. It also adds somewhat of an element of surprise to the violator because he is expecting you to come up on the driver's side.
5. You are able to see more of the passenger compartment when approaching on the right side.
6. If the subject needs to reach into his glove box or center console for some documentation you are at a better angle to see into those areas.
7. The suspect has to turn almost completely around in his seat to his right to shoot you. This is an awkward movement and physically impossible for some people. The approaching officer will see this large body movement and be able to take appropriate action.
8. Once you have obtained all of the required information return to the passenger side of your vehicle to write the ticket.
9. After you are finished writing the ticket you may want to consider going around the back of your cruiser and approaching the operator on the driver side just to mix things up a bit.

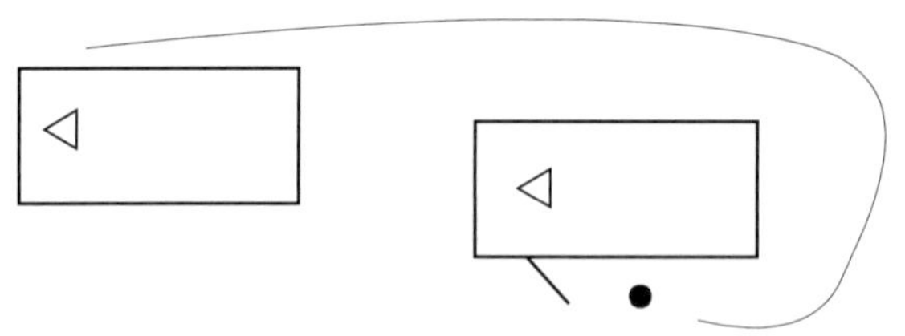

Basic Right Side Approach (Daytime)

Shadowed Left Side Approach (Nighttime)

This is a tactic that uses the shadows created by your vehicle's lights to move up on the suspect's vehicle undetected. This tactic cannot be used in a well-lighted area, as there will be no shadows for the officer to use. It should also not be used on a heavily congested highway.

1. The officer positions his vehicle in the Left Offset position slightly more to the right. The officer's left front headlight should be running down the driver's side of the subject's vehicle to illuminate the side view mirror.
2. The wigwags should be turned off and the low beams put on.
3. The officer turns off the overhead lighting to include the rotating lights and any takedown or alley lights. These lights will give the officer's movements away.
4. Any rearward facing lighting should be left on to warn approaching traffic.
5. The officer shines his spotlight into the passenger compartment of the subject's vehicle focusing on the rearview mirror.
6. The officer quickly checks for traffic before exiting his police vehicle and leaves the door to the cruiser open. The officer again checks for traffic and then takes a couple of steps to his left. This should not be conducted on a busy highway, as it will place the officer into the traffic lane.
7. The officer then moves toward the subject's vehicle utilizing the shadows as concealment. The officer does not want to be out in the traffic lane any longer than he has to so he should not waste any time in crossing the distance between his cruiser and the subject's vehicle.
8. Watch for oncoming traffic because their headlights will illuminate your position of concealment.
9. Visually inspect the trunk to insure it is closed.
10. Move in on the subject's vehicle when you are at the backseat window area. Quickly shine your light into the vehicle checking for any rear seat passengers.
11. Shine your light into the driver's eyes to ruin his night vision at the same time check his hands for weapons.
12. If you are in a two-man unit the cover officer can also take the same approach using the shadows on the right side of the vehicle for concealment.
13. Once all necessary paperwork is obtained the contact officer moves back to his vehicle to write the citation. Any cover officer will remain with the subject's vehicle.

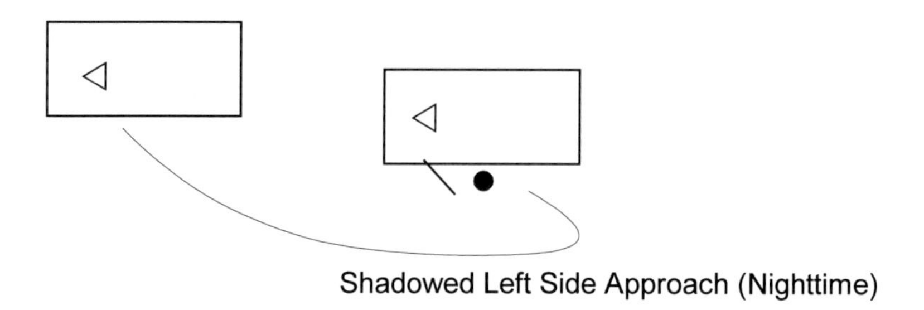

Shadowed Left Side Approach (Nighttime)

Shadowed Right Side Approach (Nighttime)

This is where the method of approaching the vehicle on the right side really pays off in a number of tactical advantages for the officer. When used properly the motorist will be taken completely by surprise. This tactic cannot be used in a well-lighted area, as it will give your movements away. However, unlike the Shadowed Left Side Approach this tactic can be used on heavily traveled roads as it does not put the officer out into the traffic lane.

1. The officer positions his vehicle in the left offset position slightly more to the left. The officer's right front headlight should be pointed in the middle of the subject's vehicle in the area of the rearview mirror.
2. The wigwags should be turned off and the low beams turned on. The wigwag lights will be to bright and will give your movements away when you move in on the vehicle from the side.
3. The officer turns off the overhead lighting to include the rotating lights and any takedown or alley lights. These lights will give the officer's movements away.
4. Any rearward lighting should be left on to warn approaching traffic.
5. The officer shines his spotlight into the passenger compartment of the subject's vehicle focusing on the rearview mirror.
6. The officer quickly checks for traffic before exiting his police vehicle and leaves the door to the cruiser open.
7. The officer crouches down and walks to the rear of his vehicle. Be sure you are ducked down low enough so your lights don't

give your movements away. The taller you are the more you'll have to duck.

8. When you reach the rear fender of your vehicle duck down even lower so the rearward lighting does not give your movements away.
9. Move around the back of your trunk at a crouch and quickly move over to the shoulder of the road into the shadows. How far over you go will depend on how much light is in the area.
10. The officer then moves towards the subject's vehicle using the shadows as concealment. You want to be far enough over onto the shoulder of the road so that you remain concealed until you move into the vehicle.
11. Watch for oncoming traffic because their headlights will illuminate you. When a vehicle approaches your position duck down out of sight using the shadows. You may have to momentarily stop your approach until the vehicle has passed. By ducking down you can use the oncoming vehicle's headlights to see into the subject's vehicle. You may not be able to see detail but you will be able to make out how many occupants are in the vehicle and whether or not they are moving around. Also if the occupants of the vehicle are looking over to their right you will know that your position has been compromised.
12. Visually inspect the trunk to insure that it is closed.
13. Move in on the vehicle when you are in the back seat window area. Quickly shine your light into the backseat looking for any rear seat passengers. (See the tinted windows section of this manual for additional details on how to use your flashlight properly.)
14. Shine your light into the subject's eyes to ruin his night vision while at the same time checking his hands for weapons.
15. If you are a two-man unit the cover officer will either "stack up" behind you and approach on the same side or he can elect to approach on the left side using the shadows for concealment.
16. Once all of the necessary paperwork is obtained the contact officer moves back to the police vehicle to write the citation. Any cover officer will remain with the subject's vehicle.
17. As with the Basic Right Side Approach this method keeps the officer out of the flow of traffic. Should the officer come under

fire and have to move quickly he could do so safely off to the right side of the road while moving to cover. (see the section coming under fire)

18. By staying in the shadows you will definitely add an element of surprise to the violator. If done properly the driver will be completely caught off guard by your approach. You may find that even though you are shining your flashlight into the vehicle the driver will still be looking over his left shoulder waiting for you. You will have to tap on his window to get his attention. Which usually results in them jumping six inches off of the seat into the air. When this occurs you will know that you have performed the stop correctly.
19. As with the Basic Right Side Approach you will be able to see more of the passenger compartment when approaching on this side. There have been a number of cases where officers have used this approach to discover the driver holding a weapon on his right side or shoved in between the driver's seat and the center console. Keep in mind that 90% of Americans are right-handed.
20. Because more of the passenger compartment is visible you will be better able to see into the glove box or the center console should the driver have to reach into those areas for documentation. You will be able to shine your flashlight directly into those areas whereas if you were standing on the driver's side you are shining your light into those areas crouched down and at an angle.

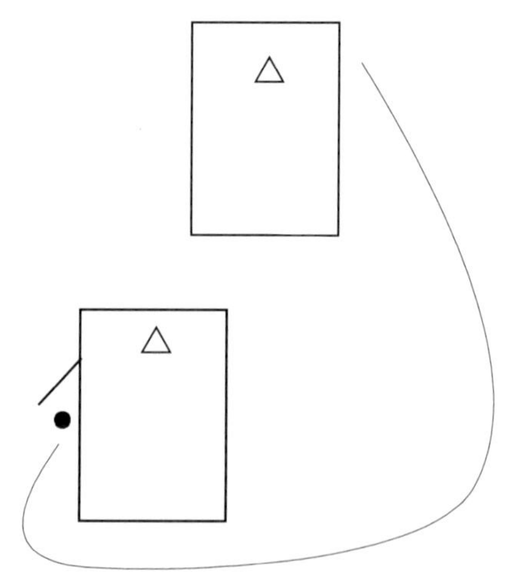

Shadowed Right Side Approach (Nighttime)

The Half Stop Approach (Nighttime)

This stop was developed to add the element of confusion with the element of surprise to the nighttime traffic stop. The more you are able to confuse and catch your adversary off guard the better chance you will have at deterring any violent actions against you. This stop can only be performed with a two-man unit and must be deployed quickly to avoid any prolonged exposure to the cover (1/2 stop) officer.

1. The patrol vehicle is positioned in the left offset position slightly more to the left. The vehicle's right front headlight should be pointed in the middle of the subject's vehicle in the area of the rearview mirror.
2. As with the Shadowed Right Side Approach (Nighttime) the wigwags should be turned off and the low beam headlights left on.
3. Turnoff all overhead lighting to include the takedown lights, rotating lights and alley lights. These lights will the give the officer's positions away.
4. Any rearward lighting should remain on to warn any approaching traffic.
5. The driver officer (cover officer) shines his spotlight into the passenger compartment of the subject's vehicle focusing on the rearview mirror. If the police vehicle is equipped with a spotlight on the passenger side then the passenger officer (contact officer) will shine that light into the passenger compartment focusing on the rearview mirror.
6. The driver officer will check for traffic before exiting his vehicle and then will exit quickly taking a guarding position standing behind his door. Both doors to the police vehicle will be left open for the entire stop.
7. The Passenger officer (contact officer) will exit the police vehicle immediately and start a Shadowed Right Side Approach on the subject's vehicle.
8. The driver officer (cover officer) will start his approach to the subject's vehicle. When he reaches the front of his vehicle he will step in front of his driver's side headlight making the outline of himself visible to the occupants of the subject's vehicle.

9. The occupants of the violator's vehicle will naturally focus their attention on the driver (cover) officer. Because of this they will not see the passenger (contact) officer approaching on the right side.
10. Timing is essential because you do not want to have the cover officer exposed in front of his headlights for a long period of time. The contact (passenger) officer should move out first and should be at the rear window area of the suspects vehicle ready to move in when the cover (driver) officer steps in front of the headlights. If the contact officer sees any danger he will shout out a warning to the cover officer.
11. The passenger officer will make contact with the driver using the same tactics that were outlined earlier.
12. Once contact has been made the driver (cover) officer will quickly cross in between the two vehicles and take up a position of cover at the right rear of the subject's vehicle.
13. When all of the necessary paperwork has been obtained the contact officer will return to the police vehicle to write the citation. The cover (driver) officer will remain at the violator's vehicle in a position of cover.
14. All other procedures of the stop will be followed as were outlined earlier in this manual.

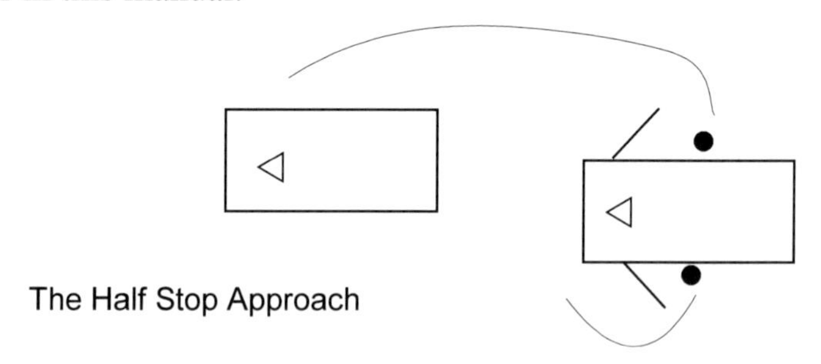
The Half Stop Approach

The Call Out

Officers need to be more cautious in their approaches to vehicles and they need to consider whether they even want or need to approach the vehicle. For this reason the Call Out stop was developed.

The Call Out stop can be deployed during nighttime or daytime patrol. It is a simple procedure where you will call the operator of the vehicle out to your position or to another location on the side of the road. This method has a number of tactical advantages to it. It is used very successfully for drug interdiction stops or for any stop that the officer for one reason or another chooses not to approach the violator's vehicle. This is not a high risk stop tactic. It is merely an extra tool for the officer to use.

The officer on any stop is responsible for the safety of everyone involved in the stop to include the violator or any of his passengers. When calling subjects out of their vehicle it is imperative that the officer takes every available precaution to insure the violator's safety. Therefore calling a person out onto a busy highway with other vehicles driving by in close proximity at high rates of speed is not advisable.

This is a good tool to use when dealing with larger vehicles such as vans, large SUV's, or vehicles with tinted windows where it is difficult to see into them. It is also a good tool to use on vehicles with multiple occupants where the officer does not feel comfortable in walking up to the vehicle but yet does not have the justification to perform a high risk stop.

This is also a good tactic to use when the subject exits his vehicle at the stop without being told to do so. Rather than order the subject back into the vehicle the officer can deploy the call out. In this situation the officer needs to be prepared for the unexpected and take charge of the situation by ordering the subject to the curb. The officer places his hand on his weapon while giving the commands as a psychological message to the violator. The message is that the officer is in charge and is willing to enforce his orders. (Command Presence) You may have some community policing oriented supervisors who disagree with this tactic. You need to ask yourself when was the last time they did a traffic stop by themselves at four in the morning with multiple suspects. Chances are you already know the answer to that question.

1. The police vehicle is placed in the left offset position.
2. All emergency lighting to include wigwags, takedown lights, rotating overheads and spotlights will be put on and directed at the violator's vehicle. This will be done whether the stop is occurring in daylight or in the dark. Even during daytime hours the police unit's lights will somewhat dazzle and disorient the subject. If the stop is occurring at night be cautious not to blind

the driver with your spotlight until he has come to an almost complete stop.

3. The driver's side spotlight should be on the left side of the subject's vehicle. This is so the light blinds him when he exits his vehicle.
4. By switching back and forth between the siren and the PA mode the PA system should already be on.
5. The driver of the police vehicle quickly checks for traffic and then immediately exits his vehicle.
6. The officer waits a couple seconds to make sure the vehicle's occupants are not exiting and then moves around the back of his vehicle. If the stop is occurring at night the officer will duck down so his movements will go undetected.
7. You can call someone out from the driver side of the police cruiser. However, it's better to be on the passenger side of the police vehicle in case you have to move to cover. (see coming under fire) If the suspect was planning on attacking you, he is going to be expecting you to be on the driver's side of your vehicle. By being on the passenger's side of your vehicle you momentarily catch him off-guard, which may give you enough time to react to the threat.
8. Once the officer reaches the passenger side of his vehicle he opens the passenger side door and obtains the PA microphone. The door should have already been unlocked with the windows down.
9. Using the PA system the officer instructs the operator of the vehicle to turn his vehicle off. He then instructs the operator to exit his vehicle and walk back to the officer's location. This is not a high risk stop so there is no need to have the driver turn around and walk backward to you. However, you do want the operator to walk slow enough to be able to do a visual frisk of the subject and to be able to read any threatening body language.
10. As the subject gets closer put the PA system down and use your voice for any further instructions.
11. From here there are two tactics that you can employ. The first one is to have the subject walk over to the curb or shoulder of the road and you can engage him from there. The second tactic is to have the subject walk to the center of your hood. The bright lights will

make it hard for him to focus on you. If the stop is occurring at night this tactic will ruin his night vision.

12. The officer can either engage the subject at the hood using the vehicle as a barrier or walk over to the curb to speak with him. Being between the two cars is a dangerous place to be should the police vehicle be struck from behind so be cautious when deploying this stop.
13. If additional paperwork is needed from the vehicle the officer can retrieve the paperwork himself or if passengers are present the officer can go to the vehicle and obtain the paperwork from one of the passengers. The driver will be placed at the rear of his trunk so the officer can watch both him and any passengers as they retrieve the paperwork.
14. The officer can also go back to the vehicle with the subject to get any additional paperwork. However extreme caution should be used here and the violator should not be allowed to get back into his vehicle.
15. Have the violator stand at the rear of his vehicle while you are writing the citation. The vehicle's lights will partially blind him and you will be able to observe his movements while writing the ticket. Do not place him back in his vehicle. If there was a weapon in the vehicle you have placed him back with the weapon. Also by keeping him out of the vehicle he will not have the opportunity to plan with any of the passengers.
16. All other procedures of the stop will be followed as were outlined earlier in this manual.
17. The benefits to this tactic are many:
    a. By calling the person out you eliminate having to walk up on someone in a vehicle that you know nothing about.
    b. Citizens are not used to this tactic so it will catch them off guard.
    c. If the subject had a plan to shoot the officer as he approached the vehicle he is now forced to revise or abandon his plan.
    d. If the subject had a plan to exit his vehicle suddenly and attack the officer he is again forced to revise or abandon his plan. If the subject ignores the officer's commands this is a good indication of where the stop is going to go and the officer needs to take appropriate action.

e. If the vehicle has any passengers this method allows the officer the tactical advantage of only having to deal with one person at a time.
f. As the subject walks back to the police vehicle the officer is given the opportunity to read the suspect's body language and to do a visual frisk of the subject looking for any bulges that may indicate the presence of a weapon. The officer is also able to see the subject's hands.
g. If the subject decides to launch an attack the officer is in a position of cover while the subject is out in the open in an exposed position where he has to deal with traffic.
h. The subject is somewhat blinded and disoriented by the patrol vehicle's lights. He has to locate you in order to attack you.
i. By using the call out method you will already have the person out of the vehicle for any field sobriety tests or arrest situations.
j. The officer is less distracted and vulnerable to passing traffic. No one wants to be fighting with some drunk in the middle of a four-lane highway. It's always better to be fighting on the shoulder of the road than in traffic.
k. On drug interdiction stops you will be able to see if the person is nervous and you will be able to read his body language.
l. On drug interdiction stops you want to separate the driver from the passengers to find inconsistencies in their story. The call out method accomplishes this by separating the driver from the passenger from the beginning of the stop.
m. You will keep him separated from any weapons that might be in the vehicle.
n. The officer has access to all of the equipment in his vehicle.
o. Should the subject decide to take off in an attempt to flee the officer can easily get to his vehicle to pursue.

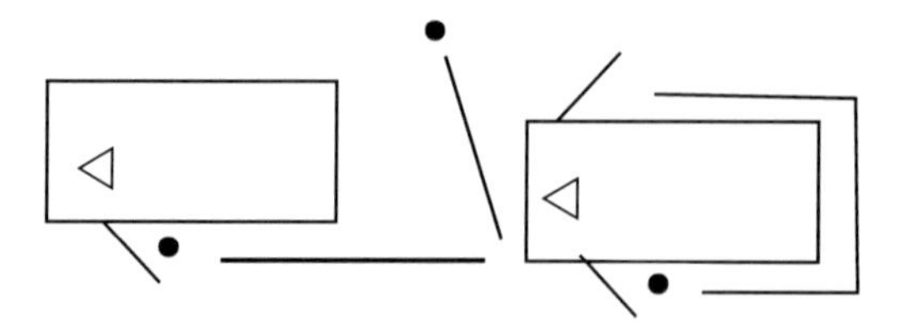

The Call Out

Termination of the Stop

Remember to be polite and professional in all your citizen contacts. The safety of everyone involved is your responsibility. This includes insuring that the vehicle you stopped gets safely back into traffic. Don't let your guard down until the stop has been terminated and the subject's vehicle is safely on its way. Remember to use caution when you re-enter the roadway. The traffic stop isn't over until the violator has left and you resume your patrol duties.

Additional Tactics

Every year officers are assaulted and murdered at traffic stops all across this country. According to the National Law Enforcement Officers Memorial Fund over 300 officers have been killed at traffic stops. Careless or intoxicated drivers struck some of the officers but over 80% of the officers were shot to death by assailants. For this reason additional tactics have been developed to assist the officer with a task that he performs on a daily basis – the traffic stop.

Having A Plan

The most important part of any traffic stop is to have a plan. Not a set plan of tactics but a flexible one that changes and adapts to the situations and problems that confront us. Flexibility and adaptability are mandatory requirements for any officer.

We all know there is no such thing as a "routine traffic stop" but yet some officers approach vehicles as if it was just another routine task with no plan of action at all. The officer needs to know exactly what he is going to do and when he is going to do it and if the suspect changes the scenario he will know exactly what to do to counter the action. The officer does this through the use of visualization. By visualizing the traffic stop and what tactics he will use the officer mentally prepares himself for the stop. He also mentally rehearses himself for the "what if" situations that can and do occur.

Listen to professional athletes or Olympic gold medalists talk about how they visualized winning the game or the event they were in. The officer needs to visualize winning the event he is in so when it comes down to saving his own life he is mentally prepared and has a plan in place to win.

Tinted Windows

Tinted windows create a unique problem for officers by providing concealment for the occupants in the vehicle. Some heavily tinted windows make it difficult to see into the vehicle even in bright sunlight. There are tactics that can be used in the day or at night to provide you with additional officer safety.

1. Use the call out method to call the operator of the vehicle back to your location. However, using the call out procedure will not allow you to see if there are other occupants or contraband in the vehicle.
2. Use your PA system to order the driver to put down all of their windows. Some rear windows may not go all the way down. This is a child safety feature placed on the vehicle by the manufacturer. However, a partially opened window will allow enough light into the vehicle to make it sufficient to see.
3. If the stop is occurring at night get on the PA system and have the driver turn on all of his interior lights. This will allow you to see into the vehicle while making it more difficult for the occupants to see out.
4. At night when using the shadowed right side approach the officer can duck down and use the oncoming headlights to see into the vehicle. Most vehicles do not have tint on their front windshields, which allows light in. You will not be able to see detail but you will at least be able to see how many occupants are in the vehicle and whether or not they are moving around.
5. When using the shadowed right side approach move into the vehicle at the right rear quarter panel/window area. Using the old FBI method of holding the flashlight up and away from your body and make contact at the rear window with your light and turn it on. This will illuminate the whole interior of the vehicle while at the same time making it difficult for the occupants to see out. But the light has to be against the glass. Use your hand to wrap around the head of the flashlight to act as a cushion. If the subjects within the vehicle were planning on shooting the officer they will shoot at the light first. The officer should be crouched down at the side of the vehicle looking through the right rear window.

Windshield Glass

Most officers don't know this but windshield glass is totally different from the glass that is in the rest of the windows in the vehicle. Officers need to be aware of this if they attempt to shoot through the windshield at a suspect. You need to know exactly where your round is going to go once it enters or exits the windshield glass.

The side and rear windows are made of tempered glass. Making tempered glass is a process where the glass is heated and then rapidly cooled. This makes the glass up to ten times stronger than regular glass of the same thickness. Which is why the glass in your vehicle is able to withstand hailstones and other impacts where normal glass would break. Bullets fired through tempered glass will stay true on target and will shatter the glass completely. However, if the glass has after market vinyl tint applied to the window the glass will shatter completely but may hold its form in the window.

Windshield glass is different in that it is made of laminated glass. Lamination is a process where a thin piece of clear or tinted polyvinyl butyral is placed between two pieces of glass. All three are then heated in a special oven where pressure is applied. This process bonds the three pieces together into one unit.

It is this makeup of the glass combined with the slope (rake) of the windshield that forces a downward drag on the bullet as it passes through the glass. The greater the rake the more drag exerted on the bottom of the bullet.

Bullets fired through windshield glass from the outside of the vehicle will drop four to six inches as they enter the passenger compartment. This is important to know because we are taught to always shoot for center mass (chest cavity) on a subject. Shooting for center mass is the quickest way of stopping the threat. If this is done the officer's bullet will drop four to six inches as it enters the windshield and will end up as an abdominal cavity hit. (see windshield diagram #1) An abdominal cavity hit isn't as incapacitating as a chest cavity hit and the subject could easily continue on with his attack against the officer. There is also the possibility that the bullet will deflect totally away from it's intended target by hitting the steering wheel or the dashboard. For this reason the officer must shoot four to six inches higher than his intended target. If you are standing outside of the vehicle and shooting through the windshield it is recommended that you shoot for the head and neck area of the individual to acquire the desired center mass (chest cavity) hit. (It should be noted that if an officer is in close proximity to the windshield the officer should angle up on the windshield to overcome this deflection. The officer has to assume the same angle as the windshield to have a true trajectory.)

The opposite is true if you are seated in your police vehicle and attempt to shoot out through your windshield. The drag is exerted on the top part of the bullet forcing your round to deflect upwards four to six inches. To overcome this problem place the muzzle of your weapon against the glass. Doing this will eliminate any upward deflection and will help in reducing the amount of glass that will be blown back from the muzzle blast. Be cautious of forcing the weapon into the windshield as you may force the slide back on your semi-auto weapon taking it out of battery.

Another problem with windshield glass is that your bullet can actually deflect or bounce off of the windshield completely. This occurs when you stand at an oblique angle of twenty-five degrees or less from the windshield forward. This area is known as the deflection zone. (see windshield diagram #2) The bullet(s) will bounce up and skim across the glass. For anyone standing on the opposite side of the windshield this could be fatal.

Another area that can effect bullet performance is the weapon's muzzle velocity. Higher-powered weapons have a tendency to stay true on target and will not be deflected. Other areas are the height of the vehicle, whether or not the vehicle is moving, how close/far back the person is sitting in the seat and the rake of the windshield.

This is not an exact science. Not all bullets will be deflected away and not all of your rounds will be deflected downwards. This is only a general rule.

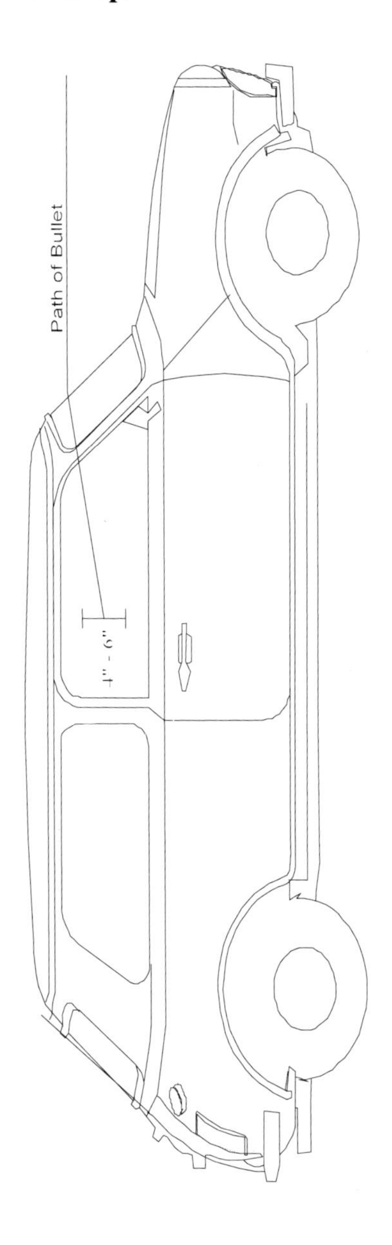

Windshield Diagram #1

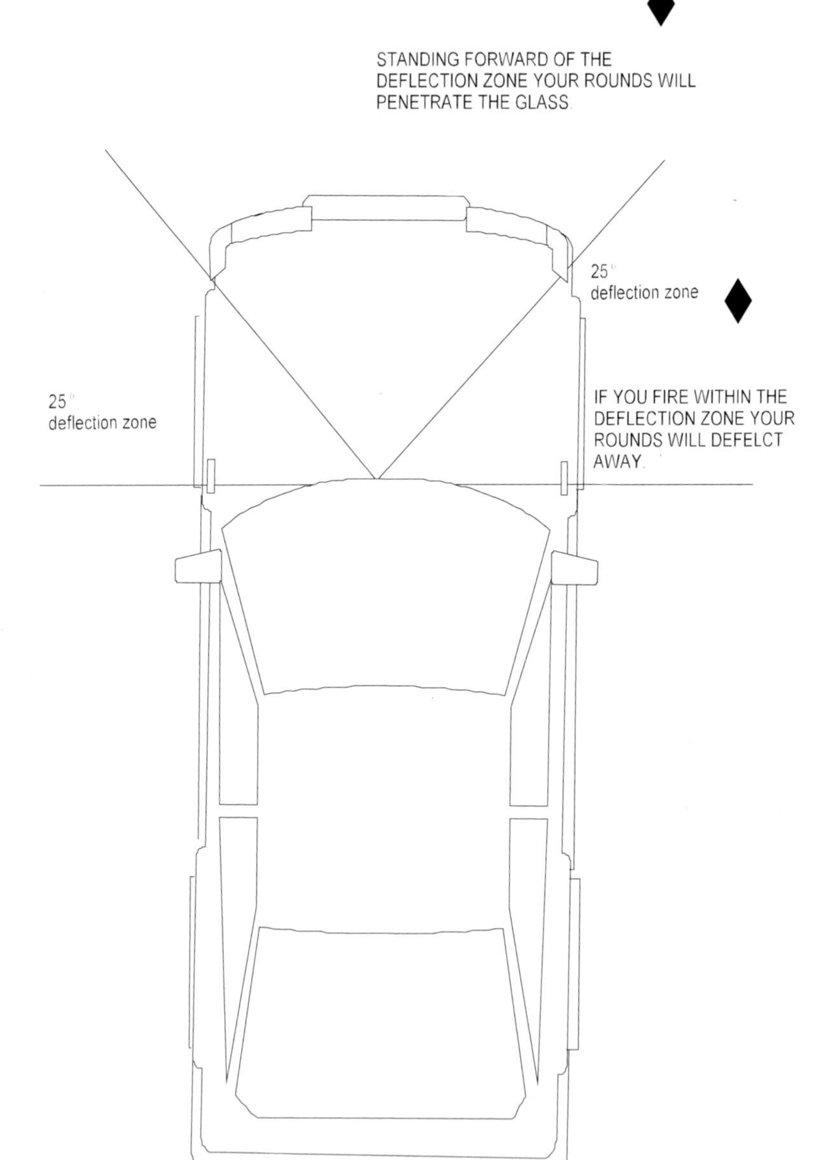

Windshield Diagram #2

Coming Under Fire

Your plan of action must also include where to go and what to do should you come under fire. The officer's tactical plan needs to be simple so it can be performed quickly and without hesitation under stress. The old military acronym of KISS (keep it simple stupid) definitely applies to officer survival tactics. Under the high stress of an officer involved shooting you are not going to be able to react to elaborate plans of action. Your plan of action needs to be simple and as with any tactic it needs to be practiced and mentally rehearsed. Keep in mind that a good plan is one that evolves with the situation and the best part of any plan is it's simplicity.

If you are faced with a lethal encounter your first plan of action should be to move and move to cover if possible while drawing your weapon. We have heard it over and over again that action is faster than reaction. With this being the case the officer is playing "catch-up" because he is reacting to the suspect's action of pulling out a weapon. The officer needs to change this around by creating some action of his own forcing the suspect to react to his action. To many times the officer tries to outdraw his adversaries trigger pull. Moving and distance are our allies. However, never turn your back on your opponent in close quarters.

Almost 95% of the officers who are able to reach cover survive the shooting incident. If you are able to survive the initial confrontation and make it to cover stay there! Wait for your backup units to arrive. If you are forced to move try to move to better cover as safely and covertly as possible.

Always look for cover at any traffic stop. Although your police vehicle does afford you some cover look for any alternate cover that may be available to you where you stop. Alternate cover could be a large tree, a brick wall or any other object that will provide you with equal to or superior cover than your cruiser. As you approach or walk back from the suspect's vehicle that alternate cover may be closer to you than your police vehicle. This may be especially true if you are performing a right side approach.

Even if you are not approaching the vehicle but are instead using the call out method you still need to look for any alternate cover that may be available to you, should you have to move.

Alternate cover allows you the mobility to move laterally rather than trying to run backwards or worse yet turning your back on your adversary in close quarters.

If no physical cover is available then psychological cover is better than no cover at all. By quickly ducking behind something the officer goes out of the suspect's line of sight. For a split second or two the suspect thinks that he cannot hit what he cannot see. An example of this would be a large bush on the side of the road. Everyone knows you can shoot through a bush. But by ducking behind the bush the officer has created some psychological cover giving him the extra time he needs to draw his weapon. Officers must keep in mind that this tactic does not always work and cannot be relied upon. But if nothing else is available "psychological cover" is better than no cover at all.

The following are some examples of where to move should you come under fire. Some of these tactics may not work for you due to the terrain; the weather conditions you work in or your own physical limitations. Consider these tactics as a general guideline. Remember to be flexible and adapt to the changes that are forced upon you.

1. In most cases you will want to have your police vehicle stopped and be out of the cruiser on your feet before the subject can exit his vehicle. Because of traffic or the location of the stop this is not always possible. You should always be prepared for any

sudden stops which would give the subject the opportunity to exit his vehicle before you can come to a complete stop. If you find yourself coming under fire in this situation try to create some distance between you and the assailant. Assume a low profile by ducking down in the seat or leaning to one side and rapidly back up and away from your attacker. Use your vehicle as cover by ducking down in the seat and return fire through the windshield. Remember to keep the muzzle of your weapon against the windshield glass while you are firing to avoid any bullet deflection and minimize the glass blow back. Your other option in this position is to exit your police car immediately while assuming cover at the rear of your vehicle and return fire. If the stop is occurring at night your emergency lighting will give you some concealment from the assailant by temporarily ruining his night vision. Look for alternate cover and move to it as safely as possible.

2. If you come under fire while you are posted at your police vehicle's door you should quickly move to the rear of your

vehicle while drawing your weapon. You can return fire from this position by shooting through your side and rear windows if you have to. Avoid shooting through your windshield at the assailant from the rear of your vehicle. From this distance the bullet will deflect upwards a considerable amount. A bullet can pass completely through a trunk so you want to keep a low profile down behind the trunk using the whole vehicle as cover. By staying down behind your vehicle, you will force the suspect to move out from behind his cover in order for him to have target acquisition to be able to shoot you.

3. Once the officer has started his walk up approach on the left side he is again in a vulnerable spot. If the officer should find himself under attack in this area between his cruiser and the rear of the suspect's vehicle he should quickly move between the two vehicles and return fire through the rear window of the assailant's vehicle. The officer should continue to move to cover behind his

police vehicle or to some preplanned alternate cover. If you have elected to perform a right side approach and come under fire in this area you will still want to move either to the rear of your police cruiser or to some alternate cover while returning fire at your assailant.

4. When you reach the driver's side door to contact the operator try to stay a little further back than you would normally stand. This will not only protect you from getting hit by the door but it will put you one step closer to the rear of the suspect's vehicle should you have to quickly backup and cut between the two vehicles. If you come under fire while at the door you should return fire at the suspect through his vehicle while quickly backing up and cutting between the two vehicles. By moving between the two vehicles the officer forces the subject to go from shooting over his left shoulder to having to turn completely around in the seat, locate the officer for target acquisition and then return fire in an awkward position. Meanwhile the officer continues to fire through the vehicle and move to cover.

Skipping Rounds

Skipped rounds are caused when a bullet hits the pavement at a low angle of 45 degrees or less from the pavement up. The bullet will actually bounce up and glide along at four to six inches above the pavement. The physics involved are similar to skipping a stone across a pond. Only because of the speed of the bullet it will only bounce once and then continue on it's path until the energy dissipates. The higher the velocity the further the bullet will travel. Officers need to be aware of this problem but they also need to realize that they can use this tactic to their advantage when a suspect is hiding under a vehicle. If the officer needs to fire at the suspect he can do so by skipping his rounds underneath the vehicle.

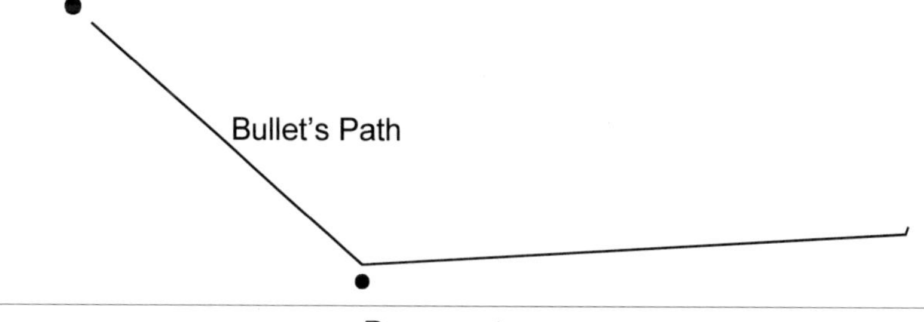

Training Issues

"Training makes the difference." This phrase cannot be emphasized enough. All of the tactics outlined in this manual should be practiced. From the basic left side approach to how to skip a bullet across pavement to shooting through windshields.

It takes very little effort to build a wooden stand to hold a windshield in to simulate the height and rake of the windshield. Go to your local auto-body repair shop or to a glass repair business and they will be more than happy to give you all of the windshields you need. Take them out to the range and set them up in your stand and fire away. Take wooden dowels to put through the holes in the glass to track the trajectory of the bullets. Find out for yourself where the rounds go. Then stand in the deflection zone and start bouncing bullets off of the windshield. Show the other officers in your agency how this is done, they'll think you were a magician. Let them think what they want at least you'll be safe from any deflected rounds coming your way.

Get a 2' x 2' piece of concrete to take out to the range to skip rounds off of. The concrete slab does not have to be very thick to successfully skip a bullet off of. Go to your local hardware store and get a few preformed concrete patio blocks. Tell them what you need the blocks for and I'm sure they'll donate them to you. Take them out to the range and start skipping rounds off of them. Place a target down range so you can see how the bullet will stay four to six inches above the ground after in bounces off of the hard surface.

Your approaches also need to be practiced. Get with your partner or another officer in your department who is as officer safety conscious as you and practice your approaches. Have one officer sit in the violator's vehicle while the other officer does the approach. Look at the stop from the violator's perspective. Look for where and when the violator can see the officer in his approach. Practice the shadowed approaches and see how close you can get to the violator's vehicle without being seen. Switch places and have your partner practice his approaches.

Now practice where to go when you come under fire. Look from the suspect's position to see where and when the suspect is able to fire on the officer. Practice moving in between the vehicles while drawing your weapon. Get an old car donated from a junkyard to take out to your range and practice moving between the two vehicles while drawing and firing your weapon.

When was the last time your department had any vehicle stop training at night? The majority of officer involved shootings occur in low light with a number of officers being assaulted and killed at traffic stops. Practice in the conditions you work in. Your training must be as realistic as possible and must simulate the conditions and environments you work in.

Go to training classes. Read the training manuals and the magazine articles that are out there. Take in as much information as you possible can. It will all pay off in the end when you need it the most. In the middle of a shootout is not the time to learn about how to get to cover.

Low Risk Motorcycle Stops

Low Risk Motorcycle Stops

Today's motorcycles are faster and more agile than they ever have been before. Because of the motorcycle's maneuverability, speed, and vulnerability it presents it's own set of unique problems when conducting vehicle stops. A motorcycle can go places that a patrol car can't. They accelerate faster than any patrol car can and they come to a stop much quicker than any other vehicle on the road.

Combine this with the fact that today's motorcycle gangs have become more organized and are more inclined to use violence to resolve their differences. A number of these gangs have resorted to armed compounds equipped with the latest in surveillance equipment and think nothing of using the pipe-bomb as a means to settle their disputes.

The majority of motorcycle enthusiasts are law-abiding citizens who enjoy the feeling of the open ride. Stereotyping an individual because of the motorcycle they ride or the protective apparel they wear is not only unrealistic but it is unacceptable. There are a number of respectable individuals who are motorcycle enthusiasts that enjoy the feeling of taking a bike down a winding road.

Initial Procedures

1. The officer must always be able to articulate the reason for the stop.
2. Because of the motorcycle's speed and maneuverability you want to take down the license tag as soon as possible. You also want to get a good description of the motorcycle, the operator and any passengers. A number of pursuits that were lost because the operator either out ran or out maneuvered the officer, or was terminated by the officer, was later solved because the passenger was found walking down the side of the road. The passenger on the motorcycle had had enough and made the driver pull over to let them off.
3. Check the vehicle's registration through dispatch. It is much easier for a motorcyclist to discard contraband on the side of the road than it is for someone in an automobile. Officers need to

maintain visual surveillance on the operator and his passengers at all times and should not be distracted by the MDT screen. If the stop is occurring at night the computer screen will impair the officer's night vision.

4. Hold off on activating your emergency lighting or closing the distance. Watch for any furtive movements on the part of the operator or his passenger. If the operator or his passengers are reaching for a weapon in their jacket or in their waistband their shoulders will give their movements away. Watch for the raising or lowering of the shoulders and or elbows. Watch for any twisting of the upper torso, which would indicate the subjects were reaching for a weapon in their waistband.
5. Consider where you want to stop the vehicle. You not only want the tactical advantages to be on your side but you want to have a safe location for the motorcyclist to pull over to.
6. Notify dispatch of your position and activity as well as the license tag number and a brief description of the bike and it's riders. If you are going to need additional resources (backup) now is the time to ask for them. If you are stopping multiple motorcycles you will want to have sufficient cover officers in place before initiating the stop.
7. Your description of the motorcycle should include any unique descriptors such as a customized paint job or any other unique descriptors of the bike.
8. Your description of the biker(s) should include the same. Example: One white male, blond hair, Mustache, mid twenties wearing a black helmet with sticker "born to ride" on back with black leather jacket.

Stopping Location

1. Choose an area well out of the flow of traffic. You want an area that gives you the tactical advantages but you also want an area that will be safe from passing cars for the motorcyclist as well.
2. Remember to choose an area that is well illuminated and familiar to you where you have a safe background for shooting.
3. The motorcyclist may not pull directly over due to loose gravel or a soft shoulder. He may either continue on until he finds an area where he feels it is safe for him to pull over onto. Or he may have

to slow down to an almost complete stop and put both of his feet down to guide the bike onto the shoulder of the road.

4. Remember that you control the stop. If you don't like the area where the motorcyclist has stopped get on your PA system and move him. Consider moving him into a parking lot or some other area out of the flow of traffic.

Pullover Procedures

1. Know your location and direction of travel before initiating the stop.
2. When you feel you are in a suitable location which gives you the tactical advantages but yet still provides a safe area for the motorcyclist to stop, activate all of your emergency lighting to include your wigwags and spotlight. Remember that even during the day these lights will somewhat dazzle and disorient the subject. If the stop is occurring at night you will want to avoid shining the spotlight on the individual until the bike has come to an almost complete stop. The light will make it difficult for the biker to see. However, you may want to shine the spotlight onto the shoulder of the road making the location of where you want the bike to stop more visible.
3. Give short blasts on your siren switching back and forth between the siren and the PA mode. This will allow the PA system to be on in case you need it. If the motorcycle is equipped with a loud exhaust the PA system may be the only way to communicate with the motorcyclist until the bike has been turned off.
4. Never pull beside the bike to pull them over or to shout instructions to the motorcyclist. This is not only unnerving for the motorcyclist but it puts the officer in a dangerous position should the subjects be armed.
5. Remember command presence. Take control of the stop and the violator.
6. Watch the riders at all times. Look for contraband being discarded or any furtive movements by the riders. Look for the raising of the shoulders and or elbows. Watch for any twisting of the upper torso.
7. If you are stopping more than one bike make sure you have enough cover officers in the area before initiating the stop.

8. Remember that a motorcycle can stop much quicker than you can so don't follow to closely.

Positioning Your Vehicle

1. You will want to be in the left offset (2'-3' to the left and 1-1½ car lengths to the rear) so you can protect the motorcyclist from passing vehicles while at the same time providing a safety zone for you if you decide to approach the bike.
2. Under normal conditions you will line the center of your cruiser with the motorcycle. If you have a partner this positioning will allow him to see the right side of the motorcycle while you can watch the left.
3. A motorcycle is much smaller than your cruiser and therefore will be able to pull further off to the side of the shoulder than you can. Don't be concerned with this positioning of the bike. Being less visible and more vulnerable than an automobile the biker may feel safer in doing this by getting completely off of the traveled road.

Pre-exit

1. Remember to roll down your windows and unlock your doors so any cover officers will have access to your vehicle for cover and or equipment.
2. Remember to turn on your portable radio before exiting your cruiser and always bring your police baton and flashlight with you.

Exiting Your Vehicle

1. Quickly check for traffic before exiting your vehicle. Then exit the vehicle immediately and take a guarding position standing by your door. Take a second or two to observe the operator and any passenger.
2. Remember to exit your vehicle as quickly and as safely as possible to give yourself more options for cover. It doesn't take much to dismount a motorcycle so don't waste any time.
3. Leave the door to the police vehicle open to force other vehicles around your position.

Approach

Once you have exited your vehicle there are three options available to you. You can do a left side approach, a right side approach or you can use the call out to have the operator of the motorcycle come back to your location.

Left Side Approach

1. Exit the police vehicle immediately and take a guarding position standing behind your door.
2. Instruct the driver of the motorcycle to turn the engine off. Have the operator and any passenger remain on the motorcycle, with the kickstand up. This forces the operator to balance the motorcycle.
3. Have the operator and any passengers remove their helmets. This is done to make communications easier. It also makes it possible to see any facial expressions so the officer can read the body language. Also a number of motorcyclist utilize two way radios with microphones built into the helmets. By having them remove their helmets you effectively cut their covert communications. Without his helmet it makes the operator less likely to take off in an attempt to flee.
4. If the motorcycle is equipped with a loud exhaust system you may have to use your PA to make your instructions understood.
5. As you approach the motorcycle you will cross in between the rear of the motorcycle and the front of your cruiser. You will want to approach the operator on the right side. This is an awkward position for the operator to be in. We want to put the operator in a position where it is difficult for him to attack you. When he is seated on his bike balancing it with the kickstand up it is difficult for him to turn to his right to launch an attack against the officer.
6. Watch for any furtive movements. The twisting of the upper torso or raising of the shoulders or elbows. Watch for items being passed from the passenger to the operator of the bike. Female motorcycle gang members are known to carry the weapons and the drugs for their male counterparts.
7. Any cover officer should remain at the police vehicle in a position of cover.

8. The contact officer obtains all required documentation (driver license, registration, etc.). This information may be contained under the seat of the motorcycle in a storage area. This storage compartment can only be accessed by lifting up the seat. Ask the operator which side the seat opens on before he lifts the seat. Most of these areas are to small to conceal a weapon in but you never know what modifications the owner may have made. Have the operator and passenger dismount the motorcycle on the hinged side of the seat. Have both subjects remain on that side of the motorcycle while you remain on the other side. Use the motorcycle as a barrier to prevent any attack. Once the required documentation is obtained instruct the operator and any passenger to remount the motorcycle.
9. If you need the motorcyclist to dismount for any other reason have him dismount on the right side of the bike. This is an awkward and unnatural movement and will put him off balance. As he is dismounting the bike to the right move around the back of the bike to the left side. Use the motorcycle as a barrier between the violator and you to thwart any assault.
10. If you feel it necessary have the operator put the kickstand up so he is forced to balance the bike once more.
11. Return to your police vehicle to write any citations. Remember to glance over your shoulder as you are returning to your vehicle. Write the citation out in the passenger side seat of your vehicle. (See the coming under fire section of this manual.)
12. Any cover officer would remain on the right side of the motorcycle in a position of cover.

Right Side Approach

1. The tactics used in the right side approach are the same as the ones used in the left side approach. The only difference is the officer moves around behind his vehicle to his passenger side door to give the instructions (turn the bike off, stay on the bike, remove your helmet, etc.). This is done to give the officer more options should he come under attack (see the coming under fire section of this manual).
2. If the subject starts to dismount the bike the officer will either use the PA system or his voice to give instructions to the subjects to

stay on the bike with the kickstand up. Once the subject's movements have been stopped the officer can then move around to the other side of his vehicle.

3. The officer then approaches the motorcycle on the right side.
4. All other tactics of the stop will be followed as were outlined earlier.

The Call Out

1. Once the vehicles have come to a stop the officer quickly checks for traffic and then immediately exits his police cruiser.
2. He takes a guarding position standing by his driver's side door for a second or two to watch the subject's actions.
3. Since the motorcyclist may already be getting off of his bike it may be necessary to give the instructions to go to the curb or the front of the police vehicle's hood from the driver's side door of your vehicle.
4. If the operator has not already dismounted have him remain on the bike.
5. While he is on the motorcycle move around to the passenger side of your vehicle. This puts you out of the flow of traffic and gives you more options for cover if you have to move.
6. Use either the PA system or your voice to call the subject either back to your location or to the curb.
7. If the subject is walked to the police vehicle the officer can either engage the subject across the hood using the hood and fender as a barrier or he can instruct the person to go over to the curb and the officer can talk to him there.
8. Once you have obtained all of the necessary paperwork have the violator remount his bike. If you feel it necessary have him put the kickstand up so he is forced to balance the bike.
9. Return to your vehicle and write the citation out while sitting in the passenger side of your vehicle.
10. All other tactics of the stop will be followed as were outlined earlier in this manual.
11. The call out is an effective tool to use when dealing with multiple motorcycles. With the call out you are only dealing with one person at a time while the others are forced to remain on their bikes with the kickstands up.

Training Issues

As with any tactic these techniques must be trained on before implementing. Find someone in your agency who owns a motorcycle or even a friend who owns a bike and practice the tactics outlined in this manual.

Have someone sit on the bike and put a weapon in his or her waistband. Watch from behind the movements it takes to retrieve the weapon so you can recognize them out in the field. Look for the twisting of the upper torso.

Put a plastic baggie in their jacket pocket and watch from behind the movements it takes to pull the baggie out of the pocket and discard it. Look for the raising of the shoulder and elbow.

Put a second rider on the motorcycle and have that person pass a weapon forward to the operator of the bike. Look from behind for the movements it takes to pass the weapon forward. Switch it around and have the operator pass the weapon back to the passenger. Practice having the passenger pull a weapon from the operator's waistband while you look at the movements from behind.

Practice the entire stop so it is committed to memory. Practice your approaches on the motorcycle. Switch places with your partner and have him/her approach you while you're sitting on the bike. Look for the vulnerable spots as well as the spots that are beneficial to you.

Sit on the bike and balance it with the kickstand up. You'll realize that it's not that hard. However, balance the bike and try to turn all the way to your right to shoot the officer approaching on the right.

Practice dismounting on the right. See how difficult it is for the rider and how unnatural it feels.

Termination of The Stop

The same procedures that were outlined earlier in the low risk automobile stops also apply to motorcycles. Be polite and professional at all times. Keep in mind the motorcycle may have the same problems getting off of the shoulder as he did getting onto it. You may have to stop traffic to allow him back into the roadway.

Low/Unknown Risk Van Stops

Vans, campers, sport utility vehicles (SUV's) and pickup trucks with caps provide a unique set of problems for the officer who stops them. Because of the vehicle's shape, size, concealment possibilities and the multiple doors and windows that need to be controlled stopping these types of vehicles can pose a hazard for the officer. For these reasons extra caution is required regardless of the reason for the stop. Remember to use Contact & Cover and remain flexible with your plan of action. Take advantage of any blind spots on the vehicle.

Low/Unknown Risk Van Stop Techniques

Initial Procedures

1. The basic procedures do not vary with a van. The difference comes with the type or model of the van. To provide tactics for your safety, you and your partner must immediately become aware of the vehicle's peculiarities: side doors, rear doors, etc.
2. Look for the type of mirrors on the vehicle. If it is equipped with concave (curved or rounded) mirrors there will be fewer blind spots if any. If the vehicle is only equipped with flat mirrors it will be easier to move up on, especially in the dark. This is only true if the vehicle is a panel style van that does not have windows running down the sides of the vehicle. If the vehicle is a mini-van or an SUV with multiple windows on the sides there will be very few if any blind spots because the operator will be able to turn around in his seat to look out a window. A pickup truck with a cap on it will have some blind spots on the vehicle and can be treated as a panel van for the purposes of the approach.

Stopping Location

The basic procedures do not vary with a van with the exception of one. You will want to have an area that will be large enough for the van to pull over on and be large enough to accommodate your vehicle to where the tactical advantages are in your favor.

Pullover Procedures

The basic procedures do not vary with a van with the exception of one.

1. The vehicle you are stopping is much larger than a regular car and may not be able to see you if you are directly behind it. For this reason you may have to pull out into the left lane so the van can see you in his side view mirrors.

Positioning Your Vehicle

1. Using the left offset position (2' –3' to the left and 15' – 25' or 1 – 1½-car lengths to the rear) still provides the best protection for the officer and the occupants of the violator's vehicle. You still want the safety zone the left offset position provides you while you are out of the vehicle. Keep in mind that the further back you are the more of the vehicle you'll be able to see. For this reason you may want to consider stopping your vehicle a little further back than the suggested distance. Remembering not to get to far back to where you can't control the stop.
2. If you have a partner in the vehicle with you some officers prefer to pull their patrol unit directly behind the vehicle and parallel to the curb leaving more room between the van and the police cruiser. This will allow you to watch the left side of the van while your partner watches the right side. The only problem with this position is that you lose the all important safety zone and now have to worry about traffic coming to close to you while you are out of the vehicle. If you prefer this method it is important that you leave your driver's door open to force vehicles around you. The left offset is still the best position.

Pre-exit

The basic procedures do not vary with a van.

Approach

The same six approaches that were outlined earlier in this manual can be used on these vehicles. The tactics do not vary with the exception that the officer is able to take advantage of the blind spots on these larger vehicles. Remember that if the vehicle has multiple large side windows or is equipped with multiple concave mirrors there will be very few (if any) blind spots.

Listed below are some additional areas that you must be concerned with when dealing with these types of vehicles should you elect to approach them rather than call the driver out.

1. As you approach the vehicle look for any side and rear doors and make a mental note of their location.
2. Visually check the side and rear doors to see if they are secure. If the pickup truck has a cap visually inspect it to insure it is closed. Do not physically check the doors, as this will give your position away to the occupants of the vehicle. Also if you open the door you may end up with the person's personal property or other equipment strewn all over the side of the road.
3. If you are performing a basic left side or a basic right side approach lightly place your hand against the side of the van. Check for movement that is not consistent with the movement of the visible occupants. If there is someone else in the van moving around you will be able to feel it.
4. While making contact with the driver either on the left side or the right side continue to check for movement in the van that is not consistent with the visible occupant's movements.
5. If the vehicle is not equipped with any side or rear windows and a cover officer is available consider having the cover officer move forward to some alternate cover to the right front of the vehicle. This will allow the cover officer a view of the interior of the van while still visually covering the contact officer. If no alternate cover is available for the cover officer then he should remain at a position of cover at the police vehicle where he can see the most of the violator's vehicle. If the cover officer where to be on the same side as the contact officer then neither one would be able to monitor the other side of the vehicle. If the cover officer and the contact officer were on opposite sides of the vehicle the cover officer would not be in a position to provide adequate cover for the contact officer. If the contact officer were to come under attack the cover officer's response would be delayed. For these reasons if there is no forward cover then the cover officer should remain at the police vehicle where he can watch the passenger

side and rear of the vehicle while maintaining partial visual cover on the contact officer.

6. If for any reason you are not comfortable with approaching the van use the call out procedures that were outlined earlier and have the person come back to your location or to the curb.

Termination of the Stop

The basic procedures do not vary with a van with the exception that the vehicle may need additional help in getting back into traffic.

Additional Tactics

If the vehicle is not equipped with concave mirrors and does not have windows on the sides there will be blind spots on the vehicle that you can use to your advantage. Below is a diagram of some of the blind spots. Naturally these spots will vary depending on the adjustment of the mirrors. For this reason the diagram should only be considered as a reference.

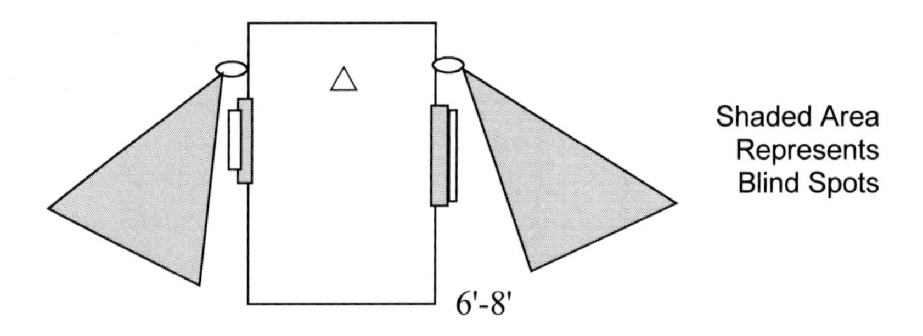

When using the shadowed approaches the officer should be far enough over to the sides to insure he is in the blind spot and then move in approximately one to two feet behind the front door. This is the biggest blind spot on the vehicle.

Training Issues

Go to a car lot and look at the vans and see how the mirrors and windows are set up. It's best to go to a used car dealer because he will have different makes and models of vans to look at. Borrow a van from someone and practice your approaches. Look for the blind spots and how to take advantage of them. Sit in the van while your partner approaches. Trade places with your partner and do your approaches on the van while he watches to see if he can determine which side of the vehicle you are coming up on.

Get a pickup truck with a cap on it and hop in the back of the truck. Look out the cap to see what your field of view is. Now hop in the driver's seat and see how much of your view is obstructed by the truck's cap.

Low Risk Bus Stops

Low risk bus stops pose a hazard not only to the police officer and the operator of the bus but to the passengers as well. Officers must take all three into consideration when weighing the benefits of stopping a bus.

A bus stop can pose a real public relations problem with passengers. To a school bus loaded with small children you are a role model and a curiosity to them. To their parents you are a delay in their child's education. To the adults on a commuter bus you are a delay in their daily activity. Possibly making them late for work or worse yet making them late getting home from work. Officers need to be as tactful as possible when dealing with buses.

Low Risk Bus Techniques

Initial Procedures

The same basic procedures apply to a bus with the exception of some added concerns.

While watching the occupants of the bus look for anything suspicious. Watch for someone changing seats around on the bus while it is moving. Most people get on a bus, sit in a seat and stay in that seat until their stop when it's time to get off. The person moving on the bus may be looking to get a better angle on you.

Watch for anyone staring at you from the bus. You may be stopping the bus for a simple red light infraction not knowing that this passenger on the bus is carrying a load of dope and is armed. In this person's drug induced paranoid mind he may feel you are stopping the bus for him.

If you are able to see up into the bus watch for passengers changing seats but leaving their bags behind. This may be a drug courier using the cross-town bus as his means of transportation. Simple observations like this can lead to some good drug interdiction work.

When considering a stopping location you will want a location that gives you the tactical advantages while still providing safety to the operator and passengers on the bus.

Your unique descriptors should include the bus number and the name of the Transportation Company or school district.

Stopping Location

The major problem with stopping a bus is finding a safe location for everyone involved. You want to select a location that gives you the tactical advantages while still providing a safe environment for everyone while you take your enforcement action. You not only have to be concerned with your safety and the bus driver's safety but you must also worry about the impatient passenger who decides to exit the bus while you are involved in your enforcement action.

A bus is a large and heavy vehicle. You will want to have a suitable location to pull the bus over on to. Look for a flat paved shoulder with enough room for the bus and your vehicle.

The driver of the bus may not pull over right away. He may be looking for a spot that he feels is suitable for the stop. If you are not satisfied at where the stop is occurring get on your PA system and move the location of the stop. If the stop is occurring on a busy highway consider moving the stop to a parking lot or a less traveled road. Be careful of this as you may be taking the bus off of its designated route.

Pullover Procedures

You are faced with the basic reality that the bus is larger than you are. Because of this you may not be that observable to the driver and will have to pull into the left lane to make your presence known.

When stopping a bus the same safety factors apply with the added safety of the passengers and the added officer safety concerns of having to watch multiple passengers.

Positioning Your Vehicle

The left offset position still affords you and the bus the best protection.

Because the bus is much larger than your police unit offsetting the unit in the left offset position may cause a hazard. Because the bus is wider you may have to pull directly behind it and parallel to the curb. By staying further back from the bus you will be able to see more of the vehicle.

Pre-exit

The basic procedures still apply with the added fact that your vehicle may be further out into the traffic lane. Because of this you will want to keep all of your emergency lighting on to warn other motorist.

Approach

Cross over behind your vehicle or walk in between the two vehicles and approach the front bus door from the curbside. The bus is a slow moving vehicle when starting from a complete stop so walking in between the two vehicles is not a concern.

Request the driver to set his brake and turn off the engine.

Have the driver exit the bus to avoid any disruption from the passengers. If it's needed have the driver come back to your patrol vehicle.

All other aspects of the approach process should be followed.

If you're not comfortable in approaching the bus use your PA and initiate the Call Out.

Termination of the Stop

The basic procedures do not vary with a bus with the exception of an arrest situation. Should you find it necessary to arrest the driver, advise dispatch to contact the bus organization or firm to send a replacement driver to you. Have someone stand by until the replacement driver arrives.

Also a bus moves slowly when first starting up so you may have to give the driver some assistance getting back out into traffic.

Blind Spots

There are several blind spots on the bus that you should become familiar with. Below is a diagram depicting these locations. The distances will vary depending on the adjustment of the mirrors and whether the bus is equipped with any concave mirrors. If the bus is equipped with large concave mirrors as some school buses are there will be very few, if any blind spots. However, because of multiple mirrors the driver will have to continuously check all of them before he locates you. Rapidly approaching or having a second officer approach from the opposite side (the Half Stop Approach) will confuse the driver and hopefully not give him enough time to react.

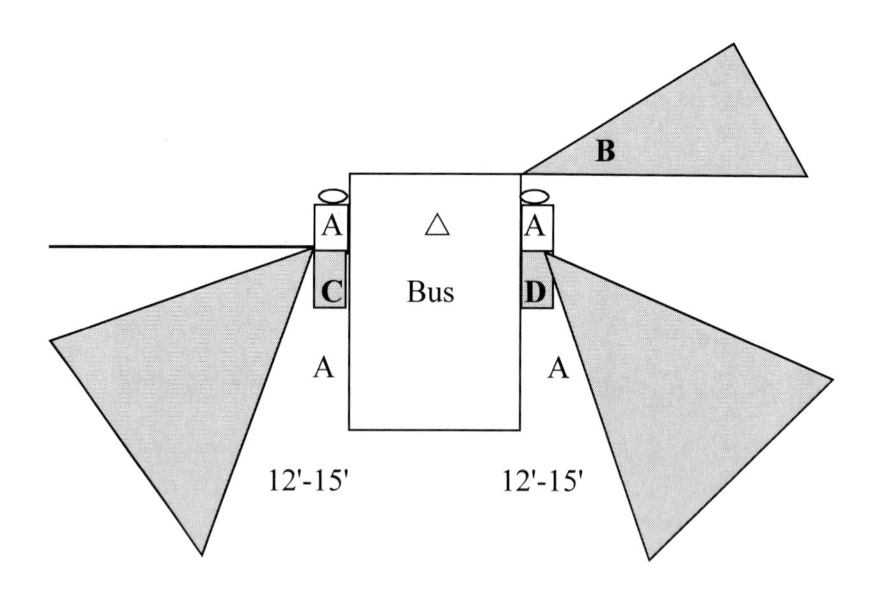

1. Position A shows the area that is visible to the driver through the side mirrors. It starts at the mirror and expands out in a cone shape to the sides and rear of the bus. The mirrors do not allow the driver to see into areas C & D. The distance at the rear of the bus will vary depending on the adjustment of the mirrors. Some

drivers prefer to see more of the rear of the bus while some prefer to see further out to their sides. The distance they can see at the rear of the bus is approximately twelve to fifteen feet from the side of the bus out.

2. Position B is caused by the windshield frame post. Because of the weight of the roof on these larger vehicles the windshield posts are much wider than they are on an automobile. This causes the driver's view to be obstructed. The View that is obstructed depends on the width of the post. If the width of the windshield post is twelve inches then the obstruction will start at twelve inches and expand out into infinity. A vehicle approaching in this blind spot can get to within a few feet before the driver can see them.
3. Position C starts approximately six to twelve inches behind the driver's window and goes to the back of the bus for approximately eight to twelve feet. Again this distance will vary depending on the adjustment of the mirror. This area is almost large enough to put a small compact car in.
4. Position D starts at the rear of the passenger door and extends to the rear of the bus approximately fifteen feet. This area is large enough to put a vehicle in. A lot of bus accidents occur when a passenger car is in this area and the bus makes a right hand turn, never seeing the car.

Training Issues

Find a bus and sit on it. Practice approaching the bus while your partner watches you in the mirrors. Look for the blind spots and learn how to approach the vehicle while taking advantage of these locations.

Low Risk Semi-Truck Stops

In a semi-truck (tractor-trailer) pullover you are faced with a situation similar to that of a bus. The vehicle's size and weight are two factors that need to be considered when dealing with these larger vehicles. Because one of these eighteen wheelers can weigh up to as much as eighty tons and exceed sixty-five feet in length you will want to have a large enough area to accommodate the tractor trailer and you.

Low Risk Semi-Truck Techniques

Initial Procedures

The same basic procedures apply to a Semi-Truck.

Stopping Location

You do have a problem with finding a safe pullover location for the Rig.

1. Try to preplan the stop location as much as possible.
2. Look for a paved flat shoulder to pull the vehicle over on to. If you pull the vehicle over onto a soft shoulder he may sink and not be able to get back out.
3. If you're on a busy highway consider escorting the Semi-Truck off of the highway and onto a less traveled roadway or parking lot. The vehicle can always be moved after the initial stop.

Pullover Procedures

1. As with a bus pullover you are faced with the same problems of size and weight. Because of the size of the truck the driver may not see you immediately. You may have to pull out into the left lane to make your presence known to the driver via his side view mirrors.
2. Even though it will be difficult to see around the Rig avoid pulling along side the vehicle. You don't want to be in any of his blind spots.
3. Don't be alarmed if the driver doesn't pull over immediately. He may be looking for a safe place for his vehicle, and you. If the

stop is made on a soft shoulder the vehicle could sink and not be able to get back out. The driver is more aware of his vehicle's peculiarities than you are. If you're not satisfied with the stopping location move the vehicle to an area that you are comfortable with.

Positioning Your Vehicle

The police vehicle's position is essentially a matter of your own preference, though the main factor to consider is always officer safety. There are three basic methods that can be used to protect you from any passing vehicles as well as providing you protection from any attack from the driver or passengers. All three positions will give you a view of the driver.

1. *The Left Offset Position*

The Left Offset Position that was outlined earlier in this manual. The police vehicle is positioned two to three feet to the left of the trailer and fifteen to twenty-five feet to the rear of the trailer. Keeping in mind that just like the van or the bus the further back away from the vehicle you are the more of the vehicle you will be able to see.

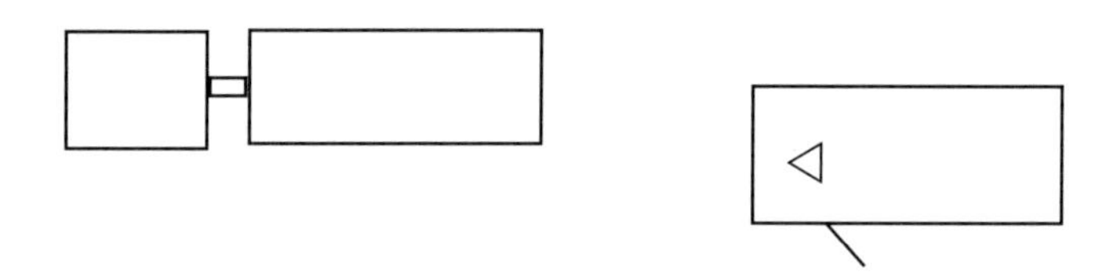

2. *The Parallel Position*

Pull in directly behind the Rig parallel to the curb. Keeping in mind that the further back you are the more of the vehicle you'll be able to see. In this position you may want to be more than the suggested distance of twenty-five feet.

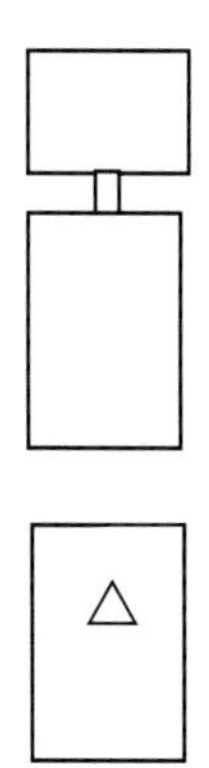

3. *The Pull Around Position*

Once the Semi-Truck has pulled over to the side and stopped, pull out around the rig on the left. Do this only when there is no traffic and it's safe to do so. Park your patrol unit about 45 to 50 feet (2½ - 3 car lengths) ahead of the rig, with the front of your unit pointed toward the right curb at a 45-degree angle. Keep in mind that traffic approaching from the rear will not be able to see your emergency lights until they are abreast of the tractor-trailer, so make sure you are far enough off of the road as to not cause an accident. From this position you can see up into the cab area. The tractor-trailer is a slow moving vehicle from a dead stop. For this reason the vehicle cannot cross the distance in time to be any real threat. The officer can easily get back into his cruiser and move it before the truck even gets close. If the officer should come under fire in this position he can use the police vehicle for cover. The officer should not move around to the front of the vehicle until he hears the air brake being set. This will be a loud release of air. There is no "park" gear so the brake has to be set.

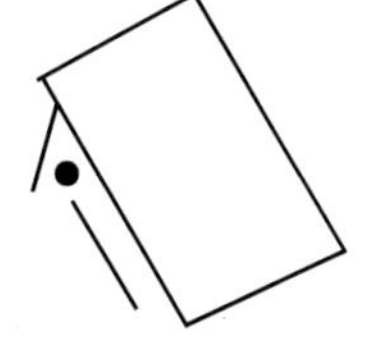

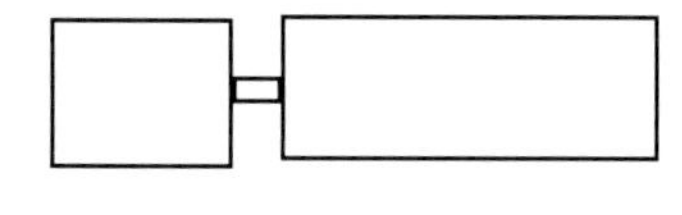

Pre-exit

The basic procedures still apply to these larger vehicles with the added fact that your police vehicle will be further out into traffic on the left offset and less visible when you pull in front of the truck. For these reasons you will want to keep all of your emergency lighting on.

Approach

The decision to approach or to call the driver out to you is based on officer preference or the circumstances at the time of the stop. If you call the driver out to your location remember that you are responsible for his safety. If the operator neglects to bring his paperwork with him so you can inspect it he will have to go back to the cab to retrieve it. If you elect to go back to the cab with the driver be cautious.

1. You can call the driver out to your location from any of the three positions that were stated previously.
   a. In the off set or parallel positions you will approach the semi on the driver's side moving no closer than the left rear of the trailer. From this position you can call the driver back to your location by motioning with your hand. If you were to come under fire in this location you can easily use the back of the trailer as cover and move to the rear or side for better cover.
   b. In the pull around position you will exit your vehicle and standing behind your vehicle motion the driver to your location. From this position you can see up in to the cab to keep an eye on any passengers while at the same time monitoring the driver's actions. If the driver exits his vehicle without his paperwork you can immediately send him back to retrieve it. If the officer were to come under attack in this position he could easily duck down behind his vehicle for cover and return fire. You have a greater reaction time with this added distance.

Shadowed Approach

2. There may be times when you will want to approach the vehicle without being seen. If this is the case use the blind spots and shadows to your advantage. However, most newer model tractor-trailers are now equipped with a number of concave mirrors that almost eliminate any blind spots. This is especially true for the cabs that are equipped with the concave mirrors on the front fenders. If you are located behind the vehicle in the left offset or

the parallel position exit your police unit and walk around the back of your vehicle. Approach the cab on the right side using the shadows and blind spots. You will not be able to see everything in the cab but you will be able to detect any movement and whether or not any passengers are present in the front seat. You more than likely will not be able to see up into the sleeper berth. From here you can instruct the driver to exit his vehicle via the passenger side door. This may not be physically possible for the driver. If this is the case then you will have to instruct the driver to exit his vehicle on the other side. You can do this by walking around in front of the vehicle to the other side or instruct the diver to meet you in front of the cab while you stay at the side for cover. Resist the temptation to climb up on the cab. This puts you at a tactical disadvantage. Listen for any release of air that will indicate the brake is being taken off.

Left Side Approach

3. If you decide to approach the driver on the left side use caution. The driver has the advantage because he has the high ground. He can see more of you than you can see of him. If you should come under fire while approaching the vehicle resist the temptation of going under the rig for cover. Unless you work on these vehicles on a regular basis you have no idea what is underneath them. The last thing you want to do if you're involved a firefight is to get hit in the head with a spare tire rack or some other piece of metal. If you try to lay down and roll under the vehicle you are limiting your mobility and wasting valuable time. Instead quickly backup while drawing your weapon and returning fire. Again resist the temptation to climb up on the rig. Instead when you contact the driver at the cab of the vehicle have him open his door so you can see into the vehicle. From here you can have the driver exit the vehicle if you wish. Have the operator move around to the front of the rig placing him between you and the cab of the truck so that you can keep an eye on him while still watching the cab with your peripheral vision.

Termination of the Stop

The basic procedures apply to tractor-trailers. Keep in mind that the Semi-Truck moves slowly at first. He made need additional time to get back into traffic and you may have to assist him with this.

Blind Spots

There are a number of blind spots on a tractor-trailer if it is not equipped with multiple concave mirrors. Remember that even with concave mirrors the driver will have to check all of them before he locates you. Below is a diagram depicting some of the blind spots on a tractor-trailer.

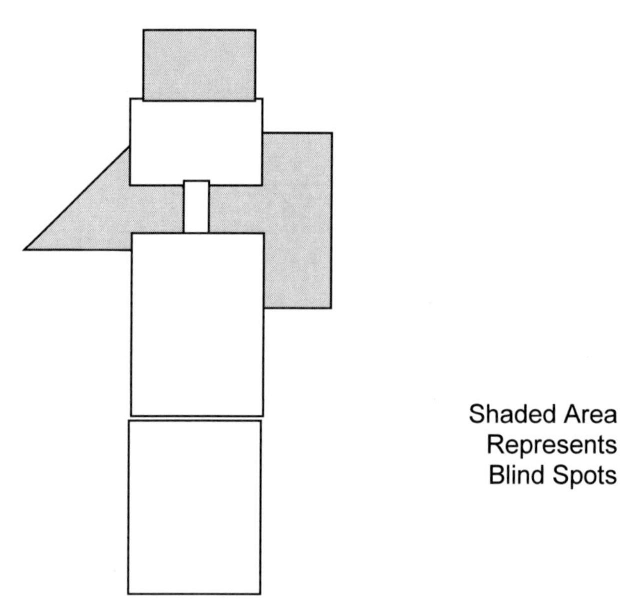

Training Issues

Go to a local trucking company or some other place that has these large rigs and sit up in one of the cabs. Look for the blind spots. Most truckers are hard working individuals and will be more than happy to assist you in showing you the blind spots on their vehicles. Look under the truck and the trailer to see how it is set up. If you are able to get one of these vehicles for training sit up in the cab while your partner approaches. See how easy or how difficult it is to spot him. Look for the blind spots and try to approach the vehicle utilizing them. Look in the cab for hiding spots where someone could conceal himself or herself in.

High Risk Stops

Definition of a High Risk Stop

Any stop which poses a significant risk to the officer when dealing with the occupants of a motor vehicle. Situations that may fall into this category are known or suspected felons, an armed individual or any potentially dangerous person.

When a police officer has a reasonable belief that a motor vehicle to be stopped contains an individual(s) that falls into this category the officer must employ a set of tactics substantially different from those used in a low /unknown risk stop. The officer's reasonable belief can be based on the officer's observations, official communications (radio broadcasts, hot sheet, Teletype information, etc.) and other sources of reliable information (reliable informant, civilian witness). You should consider the procedures outlined here as a general guideline only. You may at times find it necessary to modify these procedures in order to accommodate to your particular and unique situation. If you are forced to modify these procedures think before you act. High Risk Vehicle Stop Tactics are plans of action. These plans feature safeguards for the police, the suspect and any innocent civilians who may be in the area. Always follow your department's rules and regulations regarding High Risk Stops.

Since any vehicle stop can escalate from a Low/Unknown Risk stop situation to a High Risk Stop in a matter of seconds you should wear your ballistic vest at all times.

Understanding the High Risk Stop

High Risk Stop tactics are not to be taken lightly. You are dealing with potentially dangerous individuals who may be determined to kill you. The suspect may see you as the only thing stopping him from freedom or the rest of his life in prison. For this reason you should become thoroughly familiar with this manual and practice the tactics that are outlined in it.

In a High Risk Stop the police officer is facing potentially dangerous individuals. The suspect(s) also needs to know that he is facing danger if he does not follow the officer's orders. The officer makes this danger known to the suspect(s) through the use of command presence, immediate direction of firepower and verbal commands. The officer should practice the tactics outlined in this manual until he/she is thoroughly familiar with them before attempting to initiate a High Risk Stop.

Initial Communications

Immediately notify the dispatcher of your intentions to perform a High Risk Stop. This leaves no doubt in anyone's mind as to what you are intending to do and what resources you are going to need. At this time do not attempt to position yourself, close the distance to confirm the vehicle or extensively plan your stop.

Notify dispatch of your location and direction of travel and broadcast a description of the vehicle (plate number if available) and it's occupants. Remember to include any unique descriptors in your broadcast. Do not close the distance to obtain this information. Advise dispatch as to the nature of the stop and request your cover officers. A minimum of three officers is needed to effectively perform a High Risk Stop. A contact officer and two (2) cover officers.

Pre-Stop Period

The majority of High Risk Stops do not afford the officer a great deal of time to work out an elaborate plan for the stop. Usually this time is very short so be quick and concise in your communications. Being thoroughly familiar with the tactics in this manual will assist officers in knowing exactly what resources and tactics are needed to perform a safe and effective High Risk Stop.

Surveillance

Maintain a safe surveillance distance. The suspect(s) may think that you are not on to him. Watch for furtive movements on the part of the driver and any occupants. Look for closed windows or sunroofs being opened, passengers staring at your police cruiser, items being tossed from the vehicle, the vehicle slowing down with doors being opened for a possible "bailout" situation or any other unusual activity on the part of the driver or any passengers.

Pre-Plan Stop Location

Choose an area that affords you the tactical advantage. Stay away from intersections, hillcrests and areas that offer escape routes to the suspect(s). Try to pick an area that has good visibility and lighting with a safe background for shooting. Stay away from hostile environments where other individuals may attempt to interfere in the stop. Try to choose a less populated area to perform the stop to avoid any danger to innocent civilians.

Note: You may have little choice in where the suspect's vehicle stops. You will have to accept the disadvantages and deal with them. Being aware of these disadvantages will help in trying to minimize their effect on the stop.

Coordinate With Cover

Advise the cover officers of the location where you plan to stop the vehicle and where you want them to deploy. All officers need to know their positions so there is no confusion once the stop has been initiated. All officers involved in the stop should confirm over the radio exactly which role/position that they will be taking in the stop, with each officer involved.

Preparation

Put the windows down on your police vehicle and unlock the doors. This is done so that other officers arriving on the scene will have access to your vehicle for equipment and/or cover. Remember to undo your seatbelt just prior to initiating the stop.

The Stop

Distance: Close the surveillance distance just before the stop. Maintain a safe distance between your police vehicle and the suspect's vehicle while moving. This is done to avoid a rear end collision or stopping to close to the suspect should he stop abruptly. Gang members have been known to stop their vehicle abruptly and then reverse their vehicle at a high rate of speed. This is done to activate the airbag in the officer's vehicle disabling it. The gangbanger's vehicle then drives off. Depending on the location you want to be a minimum of 25' – 35' (1 ½ - 2 ½ car lengths) behind the suspect's vehicle when you stop. Remembering that distance is our ally, the further back you are the safer it is. However you don't want to be too far back because you won't be able to control the scene. Most urban areas will require that you be closer to the suggested minimum distance, while most rural areas will allow you to increase the suggested maximum distance. Use your best judgement for the situation that you are in.

Command Presence: Remember Command Presence. Take control of the stop, you are in charge. Activate all of your emergency lights including your takedown lights and spotlights. Illuminate the suspect's vehicle as much as possible. Activate all lights in the daylight as well. Your wigwags will somewhat disorient the suspect even in daylight hours. Activate your emergency siren. It is suggested that you do several short bursts of the siren switching back in between the siren mode and the PA mode on your radio. This will condition you to have the PA system on before you exit your vehicle. There is nothing more distracting or tiring than to try shouting over the top of your siren. Also leaving the siren on continually during the stop makes radio communications harder to comprehend.

Vehicle Positioning

Since most jurisdictions operate with one-officer units this manual will only consider that type of resource. The officer initiating the stop is the contact officer or *Primary Unit*. The second officer to arrive is the *First Cover Unit*. The third officer to arrive on the scene is the *Second Cover Unit*. If other *Additional Units* are available they will assume the positions that are assigned to them by the contact officer or the control officer. High Risk Stops are too dangerous and too difficult to be performed by a single officer, especially if the suspect vehicle contains more than one occupant. For this reason it is recommended that a minimum of three officers are needed to effectively perform a High Risk Stop, a Contact Officer and two Cover Officers. The recommended three officers is a minimum. More officers on the scene of a potentially dangerous encounter are always better. However there comes a point where too many officers could become dangerous if the possibility of a crossfire situation exists. There is also the problem of role/function duplication when to many officers are present. If the minimum of three officers is not present then the primary unit should maintain surveillance and keep dispatch informed until assistance can respond and the High Risk Stop can be effectively performed. If a lone officer is forced to make the stop then he should wait until additional officers arrive before initiating any further tactics. The officer will want to contain and isolate the suspects in the vehicle until backup arrives. Your *Verbal Commands* will establish contact and control over the suspects.

Primary Unit: The Primary Unit is the unit that initiated the stop or the first unit to arrive on the scene. The Primary Unit officer is the Contact officer initially. This Contact Officer role will interchange with the First Cover Unit officer. The Primary or Contact officer takes up a position behind his driver's side door with his handgun. The Primary Unit should stop directly in line with the suspect vehicle and should be a minimum of 25' – 35' (1½ - 2½ car lengths) behind the suspect vehicle. This position is recommended because of the advantages that it gives the officer. It insures that all of the police vehicle's lights are properly directed at the suspect's vehicle (an offset position would allow the right side of the vehicle to be shadowed). The in line position also allows the officer better visibility into the interior of the suspect's vehicle.

First Cover Unit: The *First Cover Unit* is the second unit to arrive on the scene. The operator positions his vehicle approximately 6' – 8' to the left of the primary unit at a slight inward angle. The first cover unit officer takes a guarding position behind his driver's side door and waits for the second cover officer to get into place. Once the second cover officer is in place the first cover unit officer moves around the back of his vehicle and takes up a position behind his passenger side door with his handgun. If the stop is occurring in a hostile area you may want to consider keeping this officer back as a control/rear cover officer until additional officers arrive.

Second Cover Unit: The *Second Cover Unit* is the third officer to arrive on the scene. The *Second Cover Unit* in most instances will be deployed to the rear of the primary unit, either in line with the primary unit or offset to the right of the primary unit. If the stop is occurring at night be cautious not to backlight the other officers with your headlights as you approach. This officer will deploy with a shotgun or patrol rifle behind the passenger's side door of the Primary Unit.

Control Officer/Rear Cover Guard: If you have a fourth officer present have that officer act as a *Control Officer/Rear Cover Guard.* This officer will deploy to the trunk area of the primary unit. The officer's sidearm will remain holstered while he is in this rear position behind the other officers. The duties of the control officer/rear cover guard are to have an overall picture of the stop. He is in a position to observe the actions of the other officers, the suspects and their vehicle, and the actions of any third parties that may be in the area. As a control officer/rear cover guard this officer is in control of the stop. For this reason you may want to have a supervisor in this position. The control officer can slow down the actions of the officers if the stop is going too fast. He can alert the other officers if a third party tries to intervene in the stop, and he can handle any radio communications with dispatch so that the other officers involved can concentrate on the suspects. The control officer/rear cover guard also directs any other additional units as to where best to deploy. In a hostile area this position is extremely vital.

Forward Observer(s): If cover is available and you have additional units, you may want to consider putting out a forward observer or having an officer "flank" the vehicle. The forward observer would flank the suspect's vehicle on one side or the other. Which side the forward observer decides to move up on will depend on the available cover and concealment. The forward observer's movements should be as undetectable to the suspects as possible. Giving the forward observer's position away defeats his purpose. Having a forward observer out will give you a different perspective of the vehicle and it's occupants. The forward observer would communicate his observations to the contact officer or the control officer. You must be cautious of a crossfire situation should deadly force be needed. For this reason the forward observer(s) does not take any actions on his own and must be strictly monitored by the control officer or contact officer.

Additional Units: Too many officers on the scene could cause a problem. A crossfire situation could arise, or other officers wanting to "speed things up" could create a dangerous situation for everyone involved. You may want to have additional officers assigned to traffic posts to close down any traffic on the street. If the stop turns into a barricaded/hostage situation these additional officers could be utilized to evacuate the surrounding area and set up a perimeter until other resources arrive. If additional units are available, you may want to consider strategically placing them on parallel streets. In the event of a "bail out" situation, these officers could quickly establish a perimeter making it easier to intercept the fleeing suspects.

Officers here are deploying the fan method of a High Risk Stop that can be used when there is sufficient room to position the vehicles. The center police car is the ***Primary Unit***, the police vehicle to the left of the primary unit is the ***First Cover Unit***, and the vehicle to the right of the primary unit is the ***Second Cover Unit***. We can assume that the primary unit and the first cover unit make the stop together. Once the second cover unit is in place the first cover unit officer will move into his position behind the passenger side door of his vehicle. Once all officers are in place they will have almost total visual coverage of the vehicle. This method is especially effective against larger vehicles where there is a blind spot caused by the size of the vehicle which does not allow the officers to see the whole vehicle. The suspect's vehicle should be totally flooded in light, even in daylight hours. Remember that your wigwags or any strobe lights will somewhat disorient the suspects giving you some additional officer safety by creating concealment.

The primary unit officer should always wait for his cover officers before deploying the high risk stop. However, the suspect(s) may force the officer's hand by stopping the car abruptly in an attempt to flee on foot or launch an attack against the officer. If this happens the officer will have no other choice than to deploy a high risk stop on his own to isolate and contain the suspect(s) until the cover officers arrive.

Under these circumstances the primary unit vehicle is angled to afford better protection for the officer by placing the police vehicle's engine block between the officer and the suspects in the vehicle. The police vehicle should be angled so as to allow the officer to shoot around the front of the vehicle rather than over the top of it. This alternate positioning of the primary unit is a tactical trade off wherein the officer loses some concealment from the disorienting effect of the police unit's lights but gains better cover while waiting for his cover units to arrive. Once the second cover officer unit arrives the primary unit may be repositioned to properly use the lights to illuminate and disorient the suspect(s).

This illustration shows the positioning of the second cover unit when the configuration of the roadway will not permit taking a position on the right side of the primary unit. The ***Second Cover Unit*** officer must shut off all forward emergency lighting and headlights while at the same time leaving on any rearward facing emergency lighting. Any headlights or spotlights left on will illuminate the forward officers and give away their positions of cover/concealment. The ***Second Cover Unit*** officer in the third police vehicle should take a position at the right front passenger door of the ***Primary Unit*** vehicle. If there is alternate cover available that is superior or equal to the cover that the police vehicle affords, have the second cover officer move to that position. Having a different angle of view on the suspect(s) increases officer safety. By taking a position of cover away from the police vehicles you are taking a position unknown to the suspects. This will give you the element of surprise should the suspects elect to launch an attack against the officers. This also affords the officer to have a different angle of view into the vehicle as well as a different angle of view on the suspects as they are being extracted from the vehicle. The Second Cover Officer should deploy with a shotgun or patrol rifle and needs to remain in communication with the primary unit officer.

This illustration depicts the contact officer and first cover officer in their positions. The doors to the police units are swung completely open but the officers remain in their vehicles. The windshield frame post provides some cover when shooting from this position.

It is important for the officer to understand the difference between cover vs. concealment. "Cover" will provide you with protection from incoming rounds. "Concealment" only hides you it does not stop or protect you from incoming rounds. However, concealment may temporarily provide you with some "psychological cover". By quickly ducking behind something the officer goes out of sight. For a split second or two the suspect thinks that he can not hit what he cannot see. An example of this would be ducking behind a wooden door. Everyone knows you can shoot through a wooden door. However, for a split second or two the suspect's mind thinks; "where did he go?" There is a story of a suspect who was in close quarters and was attempting to shoot an officer in the face. The officer created cover by waving his hand in front of his face. The suspect hesitated for a second giving the officer enough time to draw his weapon and fire at the suspect. Officers must keep in mind that this tactic does not always work and cannot be relied upon. But if no other cover is available "psychological cover" is better than no cover at all.

Whatever side of the vehicle you are on you should use a "strong hand" shooting position utilizing the windshield post as cover. The officer exposes more of his body but increases his accuracy by shooting with his strong hand. The majority of departments have little if any training in off hand shooting techniques. To expect an officer to use his off hand in a situation where he is under high stress and his strong hand is available is unrealistic. Both feet should be inside the Police vehicle with the outer foot braced into the doorjamb to avoid any intentional or unintentionally skipped rounds.

Some larger framed officers find this position difficult and will steady themselves by placing their outer foot on the ground with their inner foot either braced against the open door or in the doorjamb. Officers who choose this position should consider rotating their front tires fully to the left in an attempt to deflect any low or skipped rounds.

Skipped rounds are caused when a bullet hits the pavement at a low angle of 45 degrees or less from the pavement up. The bullet will actually bounce up and glide along at four to six inches above the pavement. Almost like skipping a stone across a pond. Only because of the speed of the bullet it will only bounce once and then continue on its path until the energy dissipates from the bullet. The higher the velocity the further the bullet will travel. Officers need to be aware of this problem but they also need to realize that they can use this tactic to their advantage when a suspect may be hiding under a vehicle. If the officer needs to fire at the suspect he can do so by skipping his rounds underneath the vehicle.

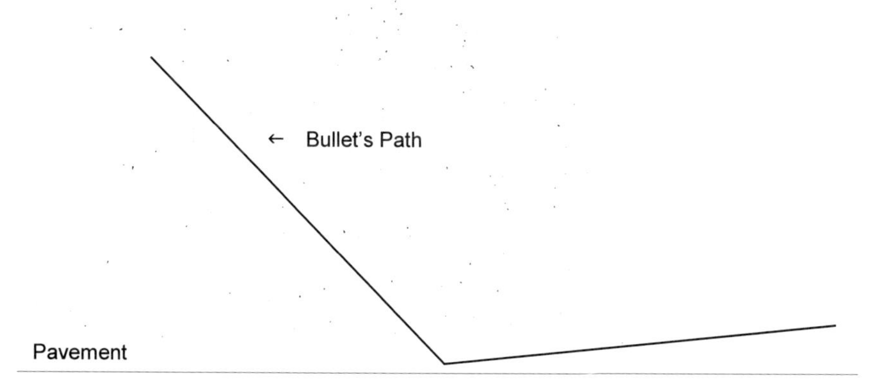

A less desirable tactic (which has been taken from Hollywood movies) has the officer exit his Police vehicle and take cover behind the opened car door. This tactic is not recommended. With cars becoming lighter every year with plastics and other lightweight materials being used to increase gas mileage the possibility of a car door stopping a round is highly unlikely. The exterior of a vehicle door is covered with a thin sheet of metal commonly referred to as a door skin, which is stretched over the door's frame. The door gets its strength from its rigidity not its thickness. Therefore the door provides little if no cover which allows most bullets, even small caliber rounds, to pass completely through the door. This tactic also leaves both legs unprotected and vulnerable to low or skipped rounds.

Another tactic has the officer kneeling behind the car door. Not only is the officer under the illusion of thinking that he is safely behind cover, this tactic is quite tiring and can be very painful for some larger officers.

Officers need to be aware of the fact that the door does not provide cover it only provides the officer with minimum concealment. The only time that a vehicle door does provide cover is when the door is equipped with a ballistic panel inserted into it. Since most departments cannot afford this luxury do not use the door as cover.

Another flawed tactic that is sometimes seen is the sideways positioning of the police vehicle. The officer either thinks he has better cover or this tactic is done to block any traffic from going around the officer. Although this position is recommended if the officer is forced into a High Risk Stop situation where he has no other choice than to initiate high risk stop tactics on his own until cover officers arrive, the officer should change the vehicle's position as soon as possible. The problem with this tactic is that it forces the officer to shoot over the car's hood exposing the officer's vital head and neck area to incoming rounds. You want to be in a position of where you are shooting around cover utilizing the angle of incidence (cutting the pie) and not shooting over cover exposing vital body parts. Although the vehicle's engine block and axles do afford the officer the best cover on the vehicle the officer has to be down behind those areas for the cover to be effective. Positioning yourself over the top of those areas will not protect you.

The **Contact Officer** in the **Primary Unit** should utilize the vehicle's public address system to communicate with the occupants of the suspect vehicle. By switching back and forth between the PA mode and the siren the PA system should already be turned on. This is important because you want to be able to give your commands to the suspects as quickly as possible. Fumbling around in your unit looking for the microphone or the PA switch wastes valuable time. Because of engine noise, traffic, car radios and a number of other distracting noises officers want to avoid shouting out at the suspects. You want your commands to be heard and understood by the suspects. Using the public address system in your vehicle will make clear communication possible. Done properly the High Risk Stop will take some time. To be yelling for that length of time will be tiring to the officer. Combine this with the high stress of facing a potentially armed individual and the rush of adrenaline that just went through the officer's system and you have an officer who will become fatigued both mentally and physically. When this happens it is difficult for the officer to stay in control of the stop.

The contact officer must perform a number of duties. He is required to focus his attention on all of the occupants of the suspect vehicle while maintaining contact and control over them through the use of the PA system. The microphone to the public address system will be in his "off hand" while maintaining a "strong hand" barricaded shooting position with his sidearm at the window post.

The contact officer needs to be aware of the possibility of a sympathetic muscle contraction. Under high stress officers have been known to have a negligent discharge of their firearm because they grabbed something with one hand and had a sympathetic muscle contraction in their other hand that was holding their firearm with their finger on the trigger. For this reason it is imperative that all officers keep their finger out of the trigger guard until ready to fire. It only takes a fraction of a second to move your finger from outside of the trigger guard to the trigger to pull it.

The First Cover unit Officer will assume a "strong hand" barricaded shooting position behind his driver's side and wait for the Second Cover Officer Unit to arrive. If it is going to be some time before the second cover officer is on the scene then the suspects must be contained and isolated in their vehicle until he arrives. You may want to consider using your shotgun or patrol rifle for added firepower until the second cover officer can get into place. Once the second cover officer is in place you should return the shotgun/patrol rifle to it's locked carrier. When the first cover officer moves to his position as a contact officer for the purposes of cuffing/control the shotgun/patrol rifle will be in the way or will end up being left unsecured while handling the prisoner(s).

When the **Second Cover Officer** arrives he should assume a position of cover/concealment behind the passenger side door of the primary unit. If the police vehicles are in the "fan position" then the second cover officer should remain at his vehicle and take a position of cover/concealment. It is very difficult for right-handed officers to shoot the shotgun/patrol rifle in the left barricade position. For this reason the second cover officer should move to the passenger side door of his vehicle if the police vehicles are in the "fan position."

Once the second cover officer is in place behind the primary unit's passenger side door, the first cover officer will move to his position behind the passenger side door of his vehicle. From this position he will act as the contact officer when it is time to cuff/ control the suspects.

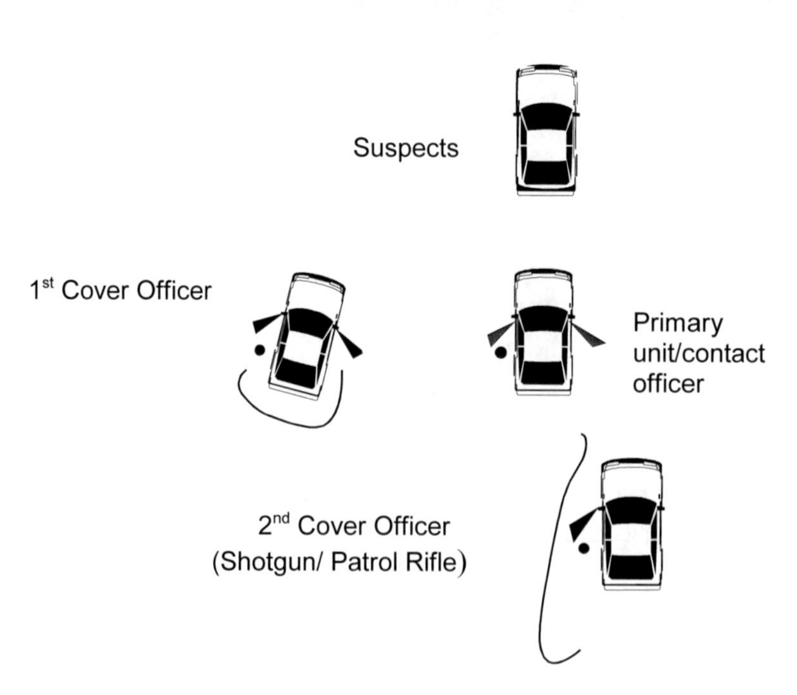

Verbal Commands

The **Primary Unit Officer/Contact Officer** has to establish control over the suspects and their vehicle from the very beginning of the stop. He does this through the use of V**erbal Commands** to the suspect(s). The officer's commands must be clear and concise so there is no misunderstanding on the part of the suspects. Using the public address system in your vehicle will assist you in amplifying your voice commands to the suspects. To avoid any confusion only one officer should give the verbal commands. Although this task is assigned to the primary officer it can be given to one of the cover officers or the control officer if the need arises. The contact officer must initially **Isolate and Contain** the suspects in the vehicle for maximum safety. The faster that the primary/contact officer is able to deploy his vehicle and direct his firepower at the suspects, the less likely they are to bail out and flee. If a suspect does exit the vehicle and flee, you must "clear" the suspect vehicle before passing it to pursue.

Example: "Occupants of the car. This is the Police. Stay in your car. Do not move. You are considered armed and dangerous. Do exactly as you are told or you may be shot."

Note: Obviously shooting the suspect(s) is not your only option. You work within a "Use of Force Continuum" which may include the use of deadly force. You must follow your Agencies rules and regulations and all State and Federal laws that govern the use of force. If the suspect is thinking about using violence against you in an attempt to kill you, you have warned the suspect that any attempt to do so may result in him being shot.

Do not order the suspect(s) to do several tasks or actions at once. Give the suspect one order and let him complete it before giving him another one. Tell the suspect when you want him to do the task so there is no surprise movement to you or the other officers involved in the stop.

Example: "Occupants of the car. Follow my orders exactly. I will tell you what to do. Do not move until you hear me say, 'Do it now.' "

Pause and repeat yourself so you are certain that the suspect(s) understand your commands. Do not rush yourself. If you have reached this point in the stop without any problems you improve your ability to control the stop by slowing down all tactics.

The primary/contact officer must **Minimize** the suspect(s) **Movement** in the vehicle. Once contained in the vehicle all suspect movement must be minimized to keep the suspects from going after a weapon. If the windows are rolled down have the suspects place their hands outside the windows so they are visible to you. Have the suspects turn their hands so that the palms of their hands are facing you. If the suspect's windows are up have the suspect place his hands on top of his head with his fingers interlaced. Some officers have the suspects in the front seat place their hands on the windshield and the rear passengers place their hands on the rear window. This tactic is not recommended due to the length of time the stop will take. The suspect's arms will become tired very quickly in this position and will lead to the suspects moving in the vehicle, which will distract you.

Example: "Occupants of the car. Stay in your car. Face forward. Put your hands on top of your head, (or out the windows). Do it now."

You want to see the suspect's hands and control his movement. Any act of non-compliance on the part of the suspect(s) should be viewed as a threat. If the suspect refuses to comply with your orders, repeat them until you have compliance.

It's recommended that you have the suspect roll his window completely down so his hands can be placed out of the window for the officers to observe. This tactic gets the suspect's hands isolated outside of the vehicle away from any weapons that may be present within the vehicle. If the vehicle's windows are not rolled down then the suspect(s) must be ordered to do so. If this needs to be done then each occupant in the suspect's vehicle must be ordered to do so separately so that not everyone is moving at once.

Example: "Driver of the car. Keep your right hand on your head. With your left hand only roll down your window. Do it now. Driver if you have electric windows roll down all of the other windows in your car. Do it now."

Once the windows have been rolled down have the driver slowly place his hands out of the window with his palms facing you.

Example: "Driver slowly place your hands out the window. Do it now. Driver turn your hands so your palms are facing me. Do it now."

The same tactics would be used on all of the occupants of the vehicle. Only deal with one suspect at a time. This decreases the risk of multiple problems that can arise out of everyone moving at once which can lead to officer distraction.

Having the suspect's hands out the window is the preferred tactic for two reasons. The first reason is to ensure that the suspect does not have a weapon in his hands. The second reason is that it makes the interior of the vehicle more visible, especially if there are rear seat passengers. When rear seat passengers have their hands on their heads it blocks the visibility of the front seat area. Obviously an exception has to be made for any center seat occupants. This person should remain seated with his hands on his head.

Note: The rear windows on some vehicles do not roll all the way down. This is a child safety feature that the manufacturer has placed on the vehicle. The rear seat passenger should still be able to get his hands out the window. Another child safety feature is the ability to lock the rear windows closed, if they are electric windows. If the vehicle is equipped with electric windows have the driver put down all of the windows in the vehicle. This procedure should be done before the engine is turned off, as the electric windows will not operate with the ignition in the off position.

After all of the vehicle's windows are down (to the extent that is possible or necessary) the vehicle's operator should be ordered to place the vehicle in park or first gear and set the emergency brake. He should be ordered to turn the ignition off and remove the keys holding them out the window. Remember to use short clear commands.

Example: "Driver of the car. Follow my orders. Put the car in park. Do it now. Driver turn the car off. Do it now. Driver set your emergency brake. Do it now. Driver with your right hand remove the keys from the ignition and hold them out the window. Do it now.

Removing Vehicle Occupants

You may come across a suspect who is wearing his seatbelt. This will have to be removed by the suspect prior to his exiting the vehicle. If you have multiple suspects in the vehicle and they all have their seatbelts on, it is recommended that you only have the person remove the seatbelt just prior to his exiting the vehicle. All other occupants should remain with their seatbelts on.

It is recommended that you remove the operator of the vehicle (with the keys) first. This tactic denies the mobility of the vehicle, and enhances the likelihood of compliance by the other occupants. You may also find that the driver may be the leader as well.

All occupants should be removed from the left side doors. This should be a standard operating procedure for all High Risk Stops to eliminate any confusion. However because of center consoles bucket seats or stick shifts it may be impossible to slide across to the left side. Even if the vehicle is equipped with a bench seat it may be impossible for the person to slide across due to age injury or size. For these reasons officers need to stay flexible and compensate for the problems. Circumstances and design dictate tactics, there is no "one answer" to cover every situation that you may find yourself in. If the occupants need to be removed from the right side of the vehicle, then all officers involved in the stop should know this before the suspects are ordered to move. Communication between the officers involved in the stop is essential. All officers should be aware of any change in tactics before they are implemented.

Your commands will be given over the public address system to the driver of the vehicle first. Make sure that your commands are clear and concise so there is no misunderstanding as to exactly what you want the suspects to do. Remember to only have the suspect do one task at a time, and wait until that task is completed before having him do another. You may want to pause between statements for clarity and effect.

Example: "Driver of the car. Follow my orders exactly. Do not make any extra movement. Do not move until you hear me say, Do it now. With your left hand only unlatch your door from the outside. Do it now. Driver with your foot, push the door open. Do it now. Driver keep your hands out of the doorway and step out of the car facing away from the sound of my voice. Do it now. Driver raise your hands high above your head. Do it now."

As the person is exiting the vehicle you should be doing a "visual frisk" of the suspect, looking for any visible weapons or any unusual bulges that may indicate the presence of a weapon. If at this time an officer sees a weapon he should communicate what he sees to the other officers. Because of the different angle of the second cover officer, he may not be able to see the weapon. If a weapon is seen the contact officer should warn the suspect.

Example: "Driver do not move. We see the gun (knife). Do not put your hands anywhere near it. Keep your hands raised high in the air. If you reach for the gun (knife) you will be shot."

At this point the driver should still be holding onto the car keys. Have the driver slip the key ring onto one of his pinky fingers. You want him to bring the keys back with him to your location for several reasons. The most important reason is to disable the vehicle. One of the other occupants of the car might have second thoughts about giving up and attempt to drive away if the keys were left in the ignition. This is a very dangerous situation where you will be trying to deal with one suspect out of the vehicle while attempting to stop the escape of other suspects. The suspects may think that if they hide or lose the keys that you are not able to search the vehicle properly. Also you may need the keys to unlock the trunk when it comes time to "clear" the vehicle. Avoid the old tactic of having the driver throw the keys out the window. This tactic will only lead to officers trying to find the keys later on, or the suspect throwing the keys where retrieval would be complicated or impossible.

When the driver is back at your location and secured you will want to inspect the keys to insure that they match the vehicle and that a phony set has not been offered.

Example: "Driver put the key ring on your left pinky finger. Do it now."

Once this is done you will want the suspect to spread his fingers open to insure that he is not holding or "palming" a weapon.

Example: "Driver spread your fingers wide open. Do it now."

From this point you will want to close the driver's door on the suspect's vehicle. This is done so that other suspects don't unexpectedly start exiting the vehicle wanting to give up. Remember that we want to isolate and contain the suspects in the vehicle and only deal with one suspect at a time. The other possibility is that the passenger could lie across the seat and fire at officers through the opened door using the vehicle as a barricade. The old tactic was to have the suspect kick the door shut with his foot. Trying to stand on one foot with your hands in the air and twist your body to kick a door shut is a difficult task for some people. Add in the possibility that the person may be under the influence of drugs or alcohol or that the person may be overweight and the task becomes even more difficult. Having a suspect fall down is very distracting to all officers. An easier tactic is to just have the suspect bump the door shut with his hip.

Example: "Driver keep your hands in the air, use your hip and bump the door shut. Do it now."

You may want to repeat yourself if the suspect doesn't understand you.

Constant communication between the contact officer and the cover officers is vital. If the contact officer is proceeding too fast the cover officers should advise him to slow down. It is only natural for the contact officer to focus or "tunnel in" on the suspect that he is directing. The contact officer needs to be aware of this and listen to what his cover officers are telling him. The first cover officer is responsible for the left flank of the suspect's vehicle and the second cover officer is responsible for the right flank. If the cover officers detect some type of actions on the part of the suspects that they feel may be a danger they will need to alert the contact officer so that he can give amplified commands to the suspects. If the cover officers were to start shouting commands at the suspects, the suspects could become confused and control would be lost. If control over the suspects is lost, then the possibility of error and injury will increase.

Once the driver has closed the door you will start the process of bringing him back to your location. You will first want to get him back away from his vehicle. You will have the suspect walk backward to the sound of your voice until he gets to about the trunk area of his car. His hands will still be raised over his head.

Example: "Driver keeping your hands raised over your head slowly walk backward to the sound of my voice. Do it now."

When the driver reaches the trunk area of his car you will give him the command to stop.

Example: "Driver stop. Do it now. Keep your hands raised over your head."

From this point a tactic that was commonly used was to have the suspect turn slowly around in a circle so that the officers could do a visual inspection for weapons. This tactic serves no real purpose and could even be detrimental to the officer's safety. The suspect should be considered armed and dangerous whether or not the officers see a weapon. If the suspect turns completely around and the officers do not see a weapon they may be lulled into a false sense of security thinking that the suspect is not armed. The other aspect of this tactic is that you have now given the suspect the opportunity to see how many officers are involved in the stop and their locations. The suspect now has target acquisition. You are using high risk stop tactics on this suspect because he may be armed and he is considered to be dangerous. Continue to treat this person as such. Do not be lulled into a false sense of security just because you don't see a weapon.

If for some reason you feel that you must have the suspect turn around, do it slowly and in quarter turns. This is accomplished by having the suspect turn to his right and then stop. Continue this process until the suspect has turned completely around.

Example: "Driver turn to your right. Do it now. Stop. Driver turn to your right. Do it now. Stop. Driver turn to your right. Do it now. Stop. Driver turn to your right. Do it now. Stop."

This procedure will give you ample time to visually inspect the suspect and stops the suspect from turning to quickly.

Keeping your hands raised over your head becomes very tiring and the suspect's hands may start to drop a little by this time. Rather than force the suspect into something that he may not be physically able to perform have him move his hands and arms into a position that is beneficial to you. Instruct the suspect to put his arms straight out to his sides. Then have him turn his palms so they are facing you. There is a saying in law enforcement training circles that the hands kill so watch the suspect's hands. Take that adage one step further in that you should watch the palms. The suspect cannot hold a weapon unless it is in his palm. A small derringer could be concealed (palmed) in his hand but cannot be hidden in his palm.

Example: "Driver put your hands straight out at your sides. Do it now. Driver turn your hands so your palms are facing me. Do it now."

This position is not as tiring for the suspect and is the best position for the officers to watch the suspect's palms.

You will now want to position the suspect so that he can be brought straight back to the area between the contact officer's and the first cover officer's vehicles. This may mean having the suspect take a few steps to his left or right.

Example: "Driver keep your hands where they are and take two steps to your right. Do it now."

You are now ready to have the suspect walk back to you. The suspect should continue to face forward and slowly walk backward to your position.

Example: "Driver do not turn around. Slowly walk backward to the sound of my voice. Do it now."

You may find it necessary to stop the suspect and have him take a few steps to his left or right to adjust his progress. Due to the terrain it may also be necessary to tell the suspect exactly how many steps to take. If the suspect is walking too fast you will want to stop him, and then start over again slower.

Continue to walk the suspect back until he reaches a point approximately six – eight feet (6' – 8') in front of the police cruisers.

This is the point where the role of contact officer switches over to the first cover officer. The first cover officer now becomes the contact officer for the purposes of cuffing/control of this suspect. The first cover officer remains in his vehicle for cover and orders the suspect to continue walking backward to the sound of his voice. The public address system should not be used at this time. The commands should only be given loud enough for the suspect to hear and not the occupants of the suspect's vehicle. The suspect should be brought back in between the two patrol cars and told to stop when he reaches a point that is even with the vehicle's front wheels. The driver will then be told (in a hushed voice) to get into a kneeling position and cross his ankles. He will then be ordered to sit back on his ankles and interlace his fingers on top of his head. The cuffing/control officer should not leave his position of cover behind his passenger side door until the suspect is in this position of compliance.

When the suspect is in this position of compliance the first cover officer will holster his weapon and move out at a low crouch to speed cuff the suspect and take control of him. If the suspect starts to offer any type of resistance or tries to reach for a weapon the cuffing/control officer should disengage from the suspect and seek cover back at his vehicle and take the appropriate action to stop the threat.

The officer will quickly search the suspect's waistband area to include the small of his back and his pockets for weapons. This should be done while the officer is holding onto the handcuffs that are on the suspect. You will want to remain in the low crouch position down behind the suspect at all times.

You should then help the suspect up to his feet and walk him backward to the rear trunk of the patrol car. Try to make yourself as small a target as possible while you are escorting the prisoner.

Take the suspect back to the trunk area of one of the patrol cars. Put the suspect into a kneeling position behind the patrol car using it as cover and thoroughly search the suspect. While searching the suspect he should be debriefed as to the number of occupants that are left in the vehicle, any weapons that are present, and the contents of the trunk. Once the suspect has been thoroughly searched he should be secured in one of the patrol vehicles. Try to keep the suspects separated in different patrol cars. Any weapons that were found on the suspects should be secured in the trunk of a patrol vehicle.

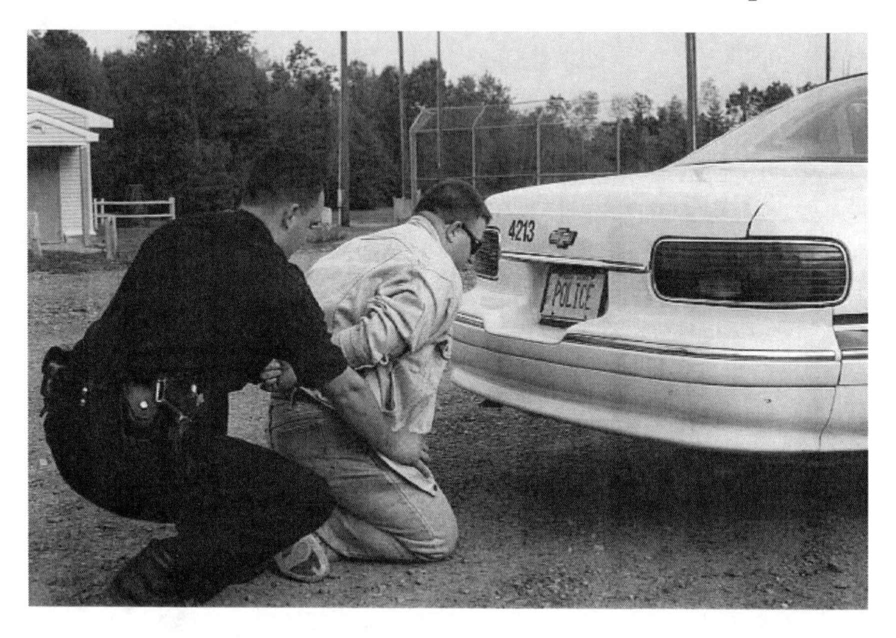

The remaining occupants of the suspect vehicle should be removed in the same manner. The ideal order of extraction is the operator, front seat middle, front seat right, rear seat left, rear seat middle, rear seat right. All of the occupants should be taken out of the vehicle on the left side and the door should be closed behind each one after they exit with the exception of the last passenger. The last passenger will leave the door open so the vehicle can be cleared. If the vehicle is only equipped with two doors the rear seat passengers may have to use both hands to exit the vehicle. Be alert to this and have the suspects exit the rear seat slowly. This is where the forward observer's position comes into play. Because of his different angle on the suspect's vehicle he should be able to see into the vehicle and watch the occupants closely.

Areas of Concern

Non-Compliance: Be alert to any conspicuous ignoring on the part of the suspects. This is a danger cue that should not be ignored. If the suspect refuses to follow your commands maintain cover and call for additional resources. Sometimes the suspect will exit the vehicle but not follow other commands given. He may be trying to figure out a way to launch an attack against the officers. If this is the case then prone the suspect out with his head turned away from his vehicle and away from your position. Once this person is put into the prone position then the contact officer will start the removal of the other suspects in the vehicle. If you have additional officers available assign an officer to cover the suspect that is prone. This will limit the distracting effect that this suspect will have. If additional suspects refuse to comply then prone them out also. Take all compliant suspects into custody first and then reissue commands to the prone suspect (s). The suspect may now be willing to comply with your commands. If the suspect still refuses to comply then leave him in the prone position until the vehicle is cleared. Do not attempt to take him into custody until the vehicle is cleared. Use contact and cover tactics when moving up on the suspect and his vehicle.

Fleeing Suspect (s): You may encounter a High Risk Stop where the suspects will flee the vehicle. A number of suspects are now fleeing while the vehicle is still moving at a low speed, leaving the police to handle the unoccupied vehicle. This tactic is becoming more popular among street criminals. Hopefully you have been able to plan the stop somewhat and have officers positioned ahead of the stop location, which would allow them to set up a perimeter. If this is the case then you will be able to broadcast a description of the suspect(s) to the officers. Never run after the suspect until the vehicle has been cleared. Street gangs have used this tactic in the past where one suspect flees while the other suspect remains in the vehicle to ambush the pursuing officer as he runs by.

If visible occupants remain in the vehicle then you will have to remain in your position of cover and continue with High Risk Stop tactics to remove them. If the suspect's vehicle appears to be unoccupied then you are faced with a couple of choices. One is to issue a "bluff callout" to the vehicle ordering any occupants to give up. Your other option is to clear and disable the suspect's vehicle before initiating any foot pursuit. Both of these tactics are discussed in detail in the **Clearing the Vehicle** section of this manual. You must also consider the possibility that the suspect(s) have not fled very far. This may be a ploy on their part to set you up for an attack or ambush situation.

The suspects may conceal themselves around a corner and wait to ambush you as you chase after them. Or the suspects may just be exiting the vehicle to seek better cover behind a wall or tree. Another possibility is that the suspects may actually circle around and attack the officers from behind. The officers must make quick decisions in this situation. They may want to consider seeking cover away from their vehicles if that cover is superior to what the vehicle affords. If the officers seek other cover they must be conscious of any crossfire situation. The officers need to call for immediate backup to deploy against the suspect's location. If possible the officers will want to incapacitate their police vehicles before moving to other cover.

Another situation that you may encounter is a suspect who exits his vehicle and either walks or runs back to your location. A suspect may do this for several reasons. This may be a diversionary tactic to draw your attention to him while another assailant attacks you. The suspect running back to your location may be attacking you himself. The person running back to your location may be a hostage that you were unaware of. Or the suspect may just be overanxious to give himself up to the police. In any case you should be prepared to handle any of these scenarios. This is why it is so important for the Contact Officer to quickly deploy his police vehicle and direct his firepower at the suspects. Any suspects approaching the officer's position in this manner should be quickly ordered into the prone position. Another option is to stop the subject, make them turn around and put them into a kneeling position. Once this is accomplished you will have to give the Verbal Commands to the other occupants of the vehicle; hands out windows, vehicle turned off, etc. When you have isolated and contained the occupants in the vehicle, then you can either bring the kneeling/prone person back to your location or assign a cover officer to that person. You will then bring the rest of the occupants out in the same manner that was described in the section Removing Vehicle Occupants. If the suspect refuses to comply and launches an attack against you then you must take appropriate action to stop the threat. Consider moving to the rear of your Police cruiser for better cover, which also increases the distance between you and the assailant. Never order the suspect(s) back into the vehicle. If the person was a hostage and was able to escape because you distracted the hostage taker by stopping him, then you have just given the hostage back.

Plus most hostages will refuse your commands to go back into the vehicle, leaving you with the problem of what to do next. Prone the person or put them into a kneeling position while doing a "visual frisk" looking for any weapons or threatening body language. Remain flexible in these situations, hostages may not follow your commands.

Clearing the Vehicle

After all of the visible occupants of the vehicle have been removed and secured the vehicle must be cleared and secured. All of the suspects should have been debriefed about the number of occupants in the vehicle the presence of weapons and any other pertinent intelligence. Never assume the vehicle is unoccupied or move out from your position of cover until officers have physically cleared the vehicle.

Clearing the vehicle starts with the **"bluff callout"** of any unseen occupants.

Example: "You in the car, we know you are in there. Sit up and raise your hands."

This verbal challenge should be repeated several times giving any hidden occupants ample time to give themselves up. Time is on your side so don't rush this process.

Note: The purpose of clearing the vehicle is to verify that the vehicle is unoccupied. Not to confront and engage any hidden occupants.

Your **"bluff callout"** may include the use of a K-9 team. To avoid confusion or duplication of commands it may be necessary to turn the verbal commands over to the K-9 handler. This may not be feasible due to the K-9 team's distance or location. Or the K-9 team may have begun their flanking approach and do not want to give their position away. Whoever is giving the commands they should be given over the PA system. As always the verbal commands should be clear and concise, and should be repeated several times so that the suspect has ample opportunity to give himself up.

Example: "You in the car this is the K-9 team. Sit up and raise your hands or we will release the dog."

If officers believe that the vehicle is unoccupied then a K-9 team should be used to clear the suspect's vehicle. If a K-9 team is not available and the officers receive no response from their verbal challenges then the officers need to approach the vehicle and clear it. If officers really believe that the vehicle contains a hidden adversary then they should not approach the vehicle. They should maintain cover and treat the situation as a barricaded suspect and call for additional resources: K-9, SWAT, negotiators, etc.

If the officer's verbal challenge elicits no response and they feel that the vehicle is unoccupied then the vehicle must be cleared and secured. It is best to approach the vehicle from a different angle than the one that was used to call the suspects out to. This would mean moving around to the side of the suspect's vehicle. Two officers should be used as **Clearing Officers** to clear and secure the vehicle, a contact officer and a cover officer. If you have additional officers in front of the vehicle then they can be utilized for this maneuver. When dealing with larger vehicles such as a van or a camper you may want to use more than one cover officer. If you elect to use more than one cover officer then the additional cover officers will "stack up" behind the first cover officer. Any forward observers should remain in place to watch the vehicle for any movement. If no forward officers are present then the clearing officers need to flank the suspect's vehicle utilizing the best cover and circle around to the side of the vehicle. If a ballistic shield is available it should be used to maximize officer safety and effectively clear the passenger compartment by providing the officers with cover. The **Clearing Officers** should approach from the side opposite of where the occupants exited the vehicle (occupants exited on the driver's side, approach should be done on the passenger's side). However this may be altered depending on the available cover and whether or not the officers have a safe background for shooting. Cover and safety should never be compromised. All officers need to be aware of the potential of a crossfire situation that exists when the suspect vehicle is approached for clearing. Any officers who remain with the police vehicles or any other officer who is not directly involved with the clearing of the vehicle should refrain from firing on the suspect vehicle. Instead they should seek cover to avoid being struck by an errant round should the clearing officers be forced to fire. Also any suspects who are in custody should be moved to a safe location. If officers other than the clearing officers are forced to fire at the suspect vehicle extreme caution should be exercised to avoid any danger to the clearing officers. Any firing by these officers should be done only when the clearing officers have backed away from the suspect vehicle and preferably have gotten to some cover.

The Horizontal Angle of Incidence

The clearing officers need to approach the vehicle using "The Horizontal Angle of Incidence." The officer utilizes the Horizontal Angle of Incidence in the same way he would use the angle of incidence or "slicing the pie" in searching a building. Instead of angling out (or slicing the pie as it is commonly referred to) around the corner, the officer utilizes a horizontal plain to "slice" into the vehicle. By lowering yourself below the vehicle's windows you have lowered yourself below the horizontal plain, thereby concealing yourself out of the line of sight of anyone who may be "ducked down" hiding in the vehicle. For a suspect to see you he would have to give his position away by raising himself up to look out the window.

From this position the officer can "slice the pie" into the vehicle by slightly raising himself up. Only the contact officer should slice the pie into the vehicle. The cover officer should stay below the horizontal plain for concealment. It should be noted that the contact officer does not need to see if the suspect is armed or any other characteristics of the suspect, only that there is someone present in the vehicle. If any portion of a suspect's body is observed the clearing officers should disengage and seek cover. Once the clearing officers have reached cover they should again attempt to call the individual out utilizing the call out procedures that were stated earlier in this manual. If the suspect refuses to comply with the verbal commands then the situation should be treated as a barricaded suspect and appropriate resources called out.

Windshield Glass

The clearing officers should approach the vehicle together on the same side. Although you may feel you have a good crossfire pattern on the suspect vehicle should you have to shoot, by approaching on opposite sides you will actually endanger yourselves.

The problem arises out of the glass that is used in windshields. The glass in the windshield is different from the glass that is used in the side and rear windows. The glass used in the side and rear windows is made of tempered glass. The process of making tempered glass is done by heating the glass and then rapidly cooling it. This makes the glass up to ten times stronger than regular glass of the same thickness. Bullets fired through tempered glass stay true on target and will shatter the glass completely.

The windshield is different in that it is made of laminated glass. Laminated glass is manufactured by placing a piece of clear or tinted polyvinyl butyral between two pieces of glass and then heating all three together in a special oven where pressure is applied bonding them into one piece. Bullets fired though the windshield will drop approximately four to six inches as they enter the passenger compartment of a vehicle.

The danger in shooting at a windshield when officers are on opposite sides of the vehicle is that the rounds will sometimes bounce completely off of the windshield. This happens when you stand at an oblique angle of 25 degrees or less from the windshield forward and attempt to fire through the windshield. Your rounds will actually bounce off of the windshield and skim across the glass. This is similar to skipping a round off of the pavement. If an officer was on the opposite side of the vehicle when you fired the results could be fatal. This area is known as the deflection zone.

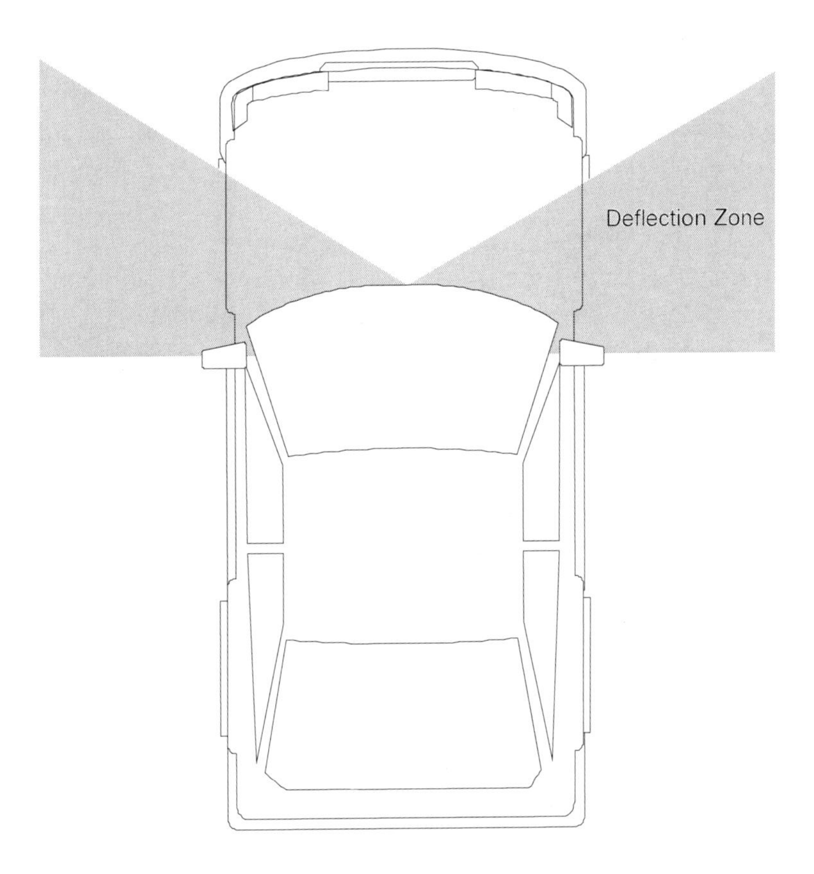

SHADED AREA REPRESENTS THE DEFLECTION ZONE

Clearing the Trunk

Once the passenger compartment of the vehicle has been cleared the officers can move to the trunk to clear that area of the vehicle. Once again if a ballistic shield is available it should be utilized to clear the trunk. A suspect has the advantage over the officers when he is concealed in the trunk. The advantage is that the suspect can get target acquisition on the officer before the officer can determine if it is appropriate to use deadly force. A suspect hiding in a trunk may be just hiding and not armed. Because of this the clearing officers must use extra caution and a special set of tactics when dealing with the trunk compartment.

You will want to have a minimum of two clearing officers, a contact officer and a cover officer. If the vehicle's trunk is equipped with an internal power release it will be to the officer's advantage to have a third officer to operate the release while two officers cover the trunk. The two clearing officers will act as cover officers while the third officer activates the trunk release button which will be on the driver's side or in the center console on some cars. All three officers should be on the same side to avoid any crossfire situation. Using the angle of incidence the clearing officers can then clear the trunk. If a ballistic shield is available it should be utilized.

If the vehicle is not equipped with an internal trunk release then the trunk will have to be manually opened by the officers. This is accomplished by having the clearing officers stand on one side of the vehicle. Which side of the vehicle they stand on depends on which side the officers approached on. If the clearing officers approached and cleared the vehicle on the passenger side then the officers will still be on that side when it's time to clear the trunk. If the officers feel they made too much noise when they approached and cleared the passenger compartment and have given away their position, then they can move to the other side.

The cover officer will very lightly place his off hand on the trunk lid to keep it from popping up and to feel for any movement. The cover officer will point his weapon downward into the trunk. Should an armed suspect open the trunk lid suddenly the officer could return fire by shooting downward into the trunk area. This downward pointing of the weapon will eliminate the possibility of the contact officer being shot by the cover officer. The officer's rounds will pass through a trunk lid.

The contact officer will already have the vehicle's keys with him that were taken from the driver earlier. The contact officer will crouch below the horizontal plain of the trunk and insert the keys into the lock. When the keys are inserted into the trunk they should be rattled but do not unlock the trunk. The rattling of the keys will alert the suspect but it may also startle him into moving. The cover officer who has his hand on the trunk lid will feel this movement. If the cover officer feels any movement then both officers should disengage and treat the subject as a barricaded suspect. You will want to debrief the other suspects who were already removed from the vehicle more thoroughly to try and obtain some information on the suspect concealed in the trunk.

If no movement is detected after the keys were inserted then the contact officer will unlock the trunk while the cover officer maintains his hand on the trunk lid to prevent it from popping up. The contact officer will maintain his crouch below the horizontal plain of the trunk and quickly move out to his right away from the vehicle and slightly towards the front taking care not to cross behind the cover officer. He will then draw his weapon and prepare to clear the trunk. The contact officer will want to give the cover officer enough room should he have to retreat.

When this is accomplished the cover officer will let the trunk lid open while at the same time moving back away from the trunk towards the front of the vehicle. By doing this both officers will be less visible to anyone hiding in the trunk. The suspect would be forced to raise himself up out of the trunk to get target acquisition on the officers. Thereby making more of his upper body mass susceptible

to taking a round fired by the officers. Also if a subject should come out of the trunk shooting he will expect the officers to be towards the rear of the vehicle. By the time the suspect realizes the officers are at the sides of the vehicle it will be to late. This will also give the officers the ability to move to the front of the vehicle for cover if need be.

The officers should wait at the side of the vehicle for a few seconds. This accomplishes several things. One is if there was someone hiding in the trunk they may become impatient and show themselves. Secondly when the cover officer releases the trunk the contact officer may be able to detect any movement that is not consistent with the trunk being opened. Also if you have a forward observer present or any rearward officers they may be at an angle to where they can see into the trunk and visually clear it.

From this point the officers will continue to work together as a team to clear the trunk. The contact officer will move to his side using the angle of incidence to slice the pie into the trunk. While the cover officer(s) stacks up beside him and aims his weapon at the trunk area. Moving together as a team will avoid any possibility of a crossfire situation. If a ballistic shield is available it should be used to clear the trunk.

Officers need to remember that they can shoot through the sides of the trunk (rear fenders) and still place an effective shot into the suspect. The outer fenders are made of the same thin metal or plastics as the door skins. Which means they provide little protection.

As with the passenger compartment if any portion of a suspect's body is seen the officers should retreat and deal with the individual as a barricaded suspect.

Once the vehicle has been completely cleared the suspects should be removed one at a time from the police cars and searched again. This is to insure that nothing was missed the first time when the officers were under considerable more stress.

High Risk Tactics for Other Vehicles

Because the criminal element within our society does not limit itself to one form of transportation officers must be familiar with the tactics needed to perform a High Risk Stop on vehicles other than an automobile. This section of the manual will discuss some of the tactics needed to perform a High Risk Stop on motor vehicles other than a car. The verbal commands as well as some of the basic tactics are the same. But because of the vehicle's size or shape other areas of concern need to be addressed to insure the officer's safety.

High Risk Motorcycle Stops

As with the High Risk Stop on an automobile the officers will want to rapidly deploy their firepower at the suspect(s) and ***isolate and contain*** the subject(s) on the motorcycle. Do not let the driver of the motorcycle put the kickstand down. Leaving the kickstand up will force the driver to balance the bike. Have the driver turn the ignition off and drop the keys at his feet. Unlike the High Risk automobile stop there is no need for the driver to bring the keys back to you.

The officer needs to ***minimize the movement*** on the part of the suspect(s). Having the subject(s) place his hands on top of his head or helmet and interlace his fingers does this. The driver of the bike can still balance the motorcycle with his hands on top his head.

As was discussed earlier in the manual, only deal with one subject at a time. Have the passenger(s) dismount first making them dismount on the right side of the bike. This is not the normal way of getting off of a motorcycle. Remember we want to disorient the suspects by making them do things that are not natural.

Bring the passenger back to your patrol vehicle in the same manner as you would in the high risk automobile stop. The majority of motorcycle enthusiasts wear protective leather so remember to be thorough in your search. Also be aware of the fact that female gang members carry weapons for their male counterparts.

Have the driver put the kickstand down and dismount him in the same manner as the passenger, on the right. From this point the officers will want to bring the suspect back to the patrol car using the high risk tactics that were outlined earlier. Some Departments teach their officers to prone the suspect out or have him kneel next to the bike. The problem with this tactic is that biker gangs have been known to conceal weapons on their motorcycles. It also forces the officer to leave cover to take the person into custody.

Once all suspects are in custody search them again to insure your safety. Because of the high stress that is involved in facing potentially deadly suspects you will want to search the subjects again once your adrenaline level has had a chance to subside.

High Risk Van/Camper Stops

Vans, campers, sport utility vehicles (SUV) and pickup trucks with caps pose a unique problem to officers in high risk stops. This is due to their sheer size and multiple doors and windows that need to be controlled. Because of these attributes it is recommended that the officers deploy using the **fan method** for high risk stops if the terrain permits it. Using the fan method will allow the officers to have total visual coverage of the vehicle.

If the officers are not in an area where they can deploy the fan method then the primary unit should deploy directly behind the suspect's vehicle. This is done so that when the second cover officer assumes his position at the primary unit's passenger side door he will be able to see the passenger side of the suspect's vehicle. Keep in mind that the further back you are from the suspect's vehicle the more of the vehicle you will be able to see.

The **first cover officer and second cover officer** deploy in the same manner as was stated earlier in this manual. The second cover officer is responsible for the right side of the vehicle. If alternate cover is available that is superior or equal to the cover that the police vehicle provides then the second cover officer should move to that cover so that he can have a better view of the passenger side of the vehicle.

If at all possible you will want to have a **forward observer** out on these larger vehicles. The forward observer will want to get some height so that he can see down into the vehicle. Because these vehicles are built with heavier materials than most automobiles and that most have interior lay outs that include center consoles, racks and other accessories that prohibit bullet penetration you will want to arm your forward observer with a shotgun or patrol rifle to maximize his firepower.

Removing the suspect(s) will be done in the same manner as was stated earlier in this manual. You will still want to have the driver exit the vehicle first with the keys. As you walk the driver backward to your location have him stop at any side doors or rear doors to unlock and open them. Have the operator move any curtains that are obstructing the view into the vehicle. Refrain from having the driver reach into the vehicle to move any large objects that are obstructing your view. Doing this may give him access to any weapons that might be hidden in the rear of the vehicle. Some vans are manufactured with a child safety feature that locks any side and rear doors automatically when the key is removed from the ignition. Any doors where passengers are visible should be left closed to isolate and contain them. Any pickup truck caps and tailgates will also need to be opened. Although opening the doors might give any hidden passengers in the vehicle an idea to flee it is better to have these doors open so that the officers can see into them as much as possible. It is much easier for a suspect to conceal himself in these larger vehicles. Any hidden subjects should be isolated and advised that the officers can see them.

Removing any passengers from the vehicle will be different from what was stated earlier mainly due to the size and style of the vehicle. It will be to distracting to the officers involved to have passengers climbing over seats and center consoles in an attempt to have everyone exit from the left side of the vehicle. For this reason it may be necessary to have the second cover officer remove any passengers from the right side of the vehicle. Once these passengers are removed from the vehicle and walked backward to the rear of the vehicle the contact officer will take over commands and direct the suspect back to the police vehicles. Your forward observer(s) should be looking for any movement from the vehicle that is not consistent with the suspect(s) exiting the vehicle.

Once all of the visible occupants are removed from the vehicle it is time to clear the vehicle. Because you left the doors open any forward observers should be able to clear parts if not all the vehicle visually. If a K-9 team is available have the K-9 clear the vehicle. If no K-9 is available then it is up to the **clearing officers** to clear the vehicle. The angle of incidence (cutting the pie) will still be used on these larger vehicles. How you approach the vehicle and from what angle will depend on the size and style as well as the interior lay out of the vehicle. You will also want to consider using more than one cover officer to clear the vehicle. If so then they need to "stack up" beside one another like a tactical team approach. Take advantage of any blind spots that may be on the vehicle. If a ballistic shield is available it should be used to clear the vehicle.

INDEX